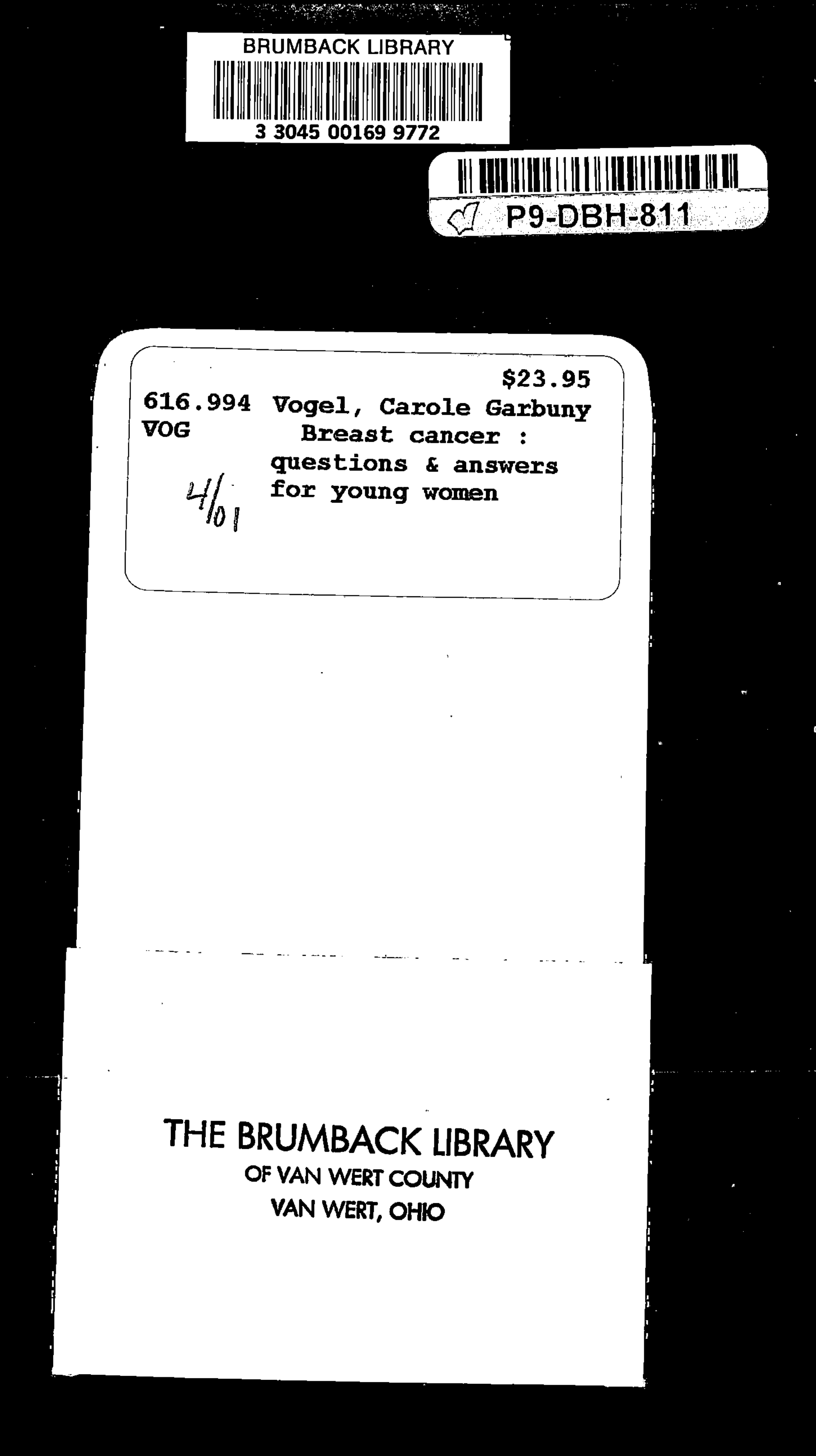

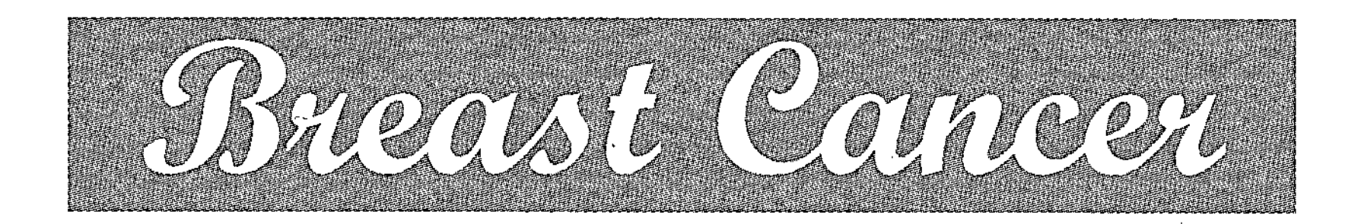

Questions & Answers for Young Women

Breast Cancer

Questions & Answers for Young Women

Carole Garbuny Vogel

Twenty-First Century Books
Brookfield, Connecticut

The goal of this book is to provide general information about breast cancer and related issues. It is not intended to substitute for the advice of a physician or other health-care professional.

Originally published in 1995 as *Will I Get Breast Cancer?: Questions & Answers for Teenage Girls* by Julian Messner, a division of Silver Burdett Press

Photographs courtesy of Photo Researchers, Inc.: pp. 32 (© A. Sieveking/Petit), 38 (© Quest/SPL), 39 (bottom: © Biophoto Associates/Science Source), 74 (Sheila Terry/SPL), 77 (© Holt Studios International/Nigel Cattlin), 84 (© Blair Seitz), 91 (© Will & Deni McIntyre), 93 (© Catherine Ursillo/Science Source), 97 (© Alexander Tsiaras/Science Source), 98 (© Alexander Tsiaras/ Science Source), 106 (© Tim Beddow/SPL), 111 (© Larry Mulvehill); Custom Medical Stock Photo: pp. 39 (top: © 1994 Richard G. Rawlins, Ph.D.), 113 (© 1991 David Weinstein & Associates); Visuals Unlimited: p. 81 (© D. Yeske); Hitachi Medical Systems America: p. 99

Illustrations by Anne Canevari Green

Library of Congress Cataloging-in-Publication Data
Vogel, Carole Garbuy.
Breast cancer: questions & answers for young women/Carole Garbuny Vogel.
p. cm.
Includes bibliographical references and index.
ISBN 0-7613-1855-0 (lib. bdg.)
1. Breast—Cancer—Miscellanea—Juvenile literature. [1. Breast—Cancer—Miscellanea. 2. Cancer—Miscellanea. 3. Diseases—Miscellanea. 4. Questions and answers.] I. Title.
RC280.B8 V639 2001
616.99'449—dc21 00—032569

Published by Twenty-First Century Books
A Division of The Millbrook Press, Inc.
2 Old New Milford Road
Brookfield, Connecticut 06804
www.millbrookpress.com

Printed in the United States of America
1 3 5 6 4 2

For Hilary Ann Barshay
in memory of her mother
Sharon Luftglas Barshay
(1955–1987)

"Her glow has warmed the world."

Contents

Although this book was written
primarily for young women,
much of the information on
breasts, cancer, risk, diagnosis,
and treatment applies to
women of all ages.

Preface

It is frightening to learn that someone you know or love has breast cancer. Most of us have mental pictures of what it is like to have cancer and what it is like to undergo cancer treatments. We construct these images from rumors we hear and from "facts" we glean from television, newspapers, and magazines. Unfortunately, these sources of information are often misleading and paint a very gloomy and depressing picture of what breast cancer is like. It's hard not to be scared by all this.

There is a way to deal with the fear, and that is with the truth. The things we imagine about breast cancer are often far worse than what is true about breast cancer. Knowledge gives you power over fear.

Some of the facts about breast cancer should be stated right now and remembered again and again:

- First, most women who get breast cancer *do not* die of breast cancer.
- Second, most girls whose mothers had breast cancer *do not* develop breast cancer themselves.
- Third, treatments for breast cancer are improving all the time.

- And finally, some of the smartest people in the world are doing research right now on early detection and prevention of breast cancer. Maybe your generation will not have to worry about breast cancer the same way your mother's generation has had to.

As you read this book, you will learn other important facts that will help you understand breast cancer and its treatments. If your mother or someone else in your life has cancer, this book will make you better able to help her and the rest of your family during these difficult times. It will probably make you feel better, too. Remember, you can beat your fears!

Barbara L. Smith, M.D., Ph.D., F.A.C.S.,
Director, Comprehensive Breast Health Center, and Co-Director of the
Gillette Center for Women's Cancers
Boston, Massachusetts

Acknowledgments

I am thankful to Barbara L. Smith, M.D., Ph.D., F.A.C.S., Director, Comprehensive Breast Health Center, and Co-Director of the Gillette Center for Women's Cancers, who took time from her busy schedule to read and critique the manuscripts for the original and the updated editions of this book. Her keen intellect, vast knowledge of the field, and compassion for her patients were reflected in her comments.

I am deeply honored that the Association for the Care of Children's Health bestowed the Joan Fassler Memorial Book Award on this book. The award is given annually for excellence in children's literature dealing with medical or health-related issues.

I am grateful to the following mental-health professionals for their time and insight: Dr. Robert S. DeIulio, licensed counseling psychologist, Wellesley Hills, Massachusetts, now retired; my sister Ellen V. Garbuny, L.S.W., Butler, Pennsylvania; and Rosalie Gerut, M.A., Milton, Massachusetts.

A special thanks goes to Joyce A. Nettleton, D.Sc., R.D., Director, Science Communications, at the Institute of Food Technologists in Chicago, for her invaluable criticisms and scientific expertise.

I am also grateful to staff of the Office of Cancer Communications at the National Cancer Institute in Bethesda, Maryland, for providing data and answering questions; my sister Vivian Prunier, Ph.D., of the Office of Pesticide Programs, Environmental Protection Agency in Washington, D.C., for contributing up-to-date information on environmental contaminants; Don Backner, radiology manager, Massachusetts Eye and Ear Infirmary in Boston, for sharing his expertise; Karen Funkenstein, a science teacher at the Winsor School in Boston, for her insight into instructing preteen and teenage girls; the American Cancer Society Media Relations Office in New York, for supplying information; the librarians at Cary Memorial Library in Lexington, Massachusetts, for their patience and help in tracking down the most obscure facts, and especially reference librarian Heather Vandermillen for providing titles for my Resources section; my former high school biology teacher, Joan Gottlieb, Ph.D., of Pittsburgh, for reviewing the manuscript; my former agent, Renée Cho, who placed the first edition of this book with Julian Messner; and my current agent, Tracey Adams of McIntosh & Otis, who found a home for the second edition with The Millbrook Press and Twenty-First Century Books. I have had the pleasure of working with two extraordinary editors, Adriane Ruggiero from Julian Messner, and Laura Walsh at Millbrook, who gave this book a second chance.

I am indebted to fellow writers Florence Harris, Susan Sekuler, and Barbara Ehrlich White for their advice and support. I am especially grateful for the input from my preteen and teenage critics, Hilary Barshay, Kate Vogel, Rachel Prunier, and Sarah Prunier, for reading the manuscript and telling me what worked and what didn't.

I would like to acknowledge the help of many other people who helped either directly or indirectly. Where the opinions of experts conflicted, I used my own judgment in presenting the information.

I would like to thank my husband, Mark A. Vogel, for his encouragement and understanding, especially when dinners became his responsibility. I am grateful to my children, Joshua and Kate, for understanding that "I'll be done in a minute" really meant, "I need another hour. Go fend for yourselves." Without the support of my family this book would have been impossible to write.

In 1987 my closest friend, Sharon Luftglas Barshay, died of breast cancer. She was only thirty-two years old and she left behind a husband, a six-year-old daughter, a four-year-old son, her parents, two sisters, a huge extended family, many friends, and me.

Sharon was a pediatric nurse. She loved children, dancing, music, traditions, and most of all, her family and friends. I miss her wisdom, her compassion, and her laughter. And I miss the person I was in her presence. I loved being her friend.

What makes me the most angry about Sharon's death is that it was probably preventable. Sharon's own grandmother had died of breast cancer, and Sharon knew that she might develop the disease when she was older. She examined her breasts regularly and one day discovered a small lump. At the time she was a nursing mother and she thought the lump was related to breast-milk production. She waited until the baby was weaned before checking it out with her doctor.

Her doctor dismissed her concerns. He said he didn't think the lump was cancerous. But the lump continued to grow, and three months later Sharon consulted a different doctor. Within days the diagnosis of breast cancer was made, and my friend's three-year battle with cancer commenced.

She never had a fighting chance. By the time treatment began, the cancer had already spread to distant parts of her body. If the cancer had been detected at an early stage, Sharon would probably be alive today.

At her funeral, I vowed that Sharon's death would make a difference. This book is a fulfillment of that promise. As I was writing it I often wondered what Sharon would think. I finally decided her reaction would be, *"Are you crazy? This book is going to scare kids to death!"* And she would be almost right.

Breast cancer is a very scary subject, and as much as I have tried, I couldn't tell you what you need to know without writing a lot of upsetting stuff. I wish I could be with you to help you through the difficult parts of this book. Since I can't, you might find it helpful to discuss worrisome parts with a parent, your doctor or nurse, or another adult whom you trust.

I have tried to anticipate your questions and your concerns about breast cancer. For easy reading, the information appears in a question-and-answer format. It ranges from the highly technical to the very emotional. You can skip over the questions that don't interest you and concentrate on the ones that do. Or you can read the book from beginning to end to get the whole picture. You can even pass over some chapters near the beginning of the book and go back to them later. Do what best meets your needs.

Chapters Four and Six are the most important. Four tells you what you can do to protect yourself from breast cancer. It also explains how you can detect the disease early, when the cancer can most easily be cured. This chapter is *must* reading even if you skip the rest of the book. Chapter Six talks about feelings and what to expect if your mother (or someone else close to you) is undergoing cancer treatment. As for the other chapters:

- Chapter One answers questions you may have about breasts and about your own changing body.
- Chapter Two describes the nature of cancer.
- Chapter Three discusses risk—the likelihood of getting breast cancer.
- Chapter Five explains how breast cancer is diagnosed and treated.
- Chapter Seven offers help if someone close to you is losing her battle with cancer.
- Chapter Eight forecasts advances in research that may make cancer easier to prevent and cure in the future.

Take charge of your health! You have an excellent chance of living to a ripe old age even with a family history of breast cancer. I hope you will find this book helpful.

Sincerely,
Carole G. Vogel

Chapter One

Breast Basics

If you are between the ages of ten and seventeen, big changes are taking place in your body. You are changing from a girl into a young woman. Your hips are getting wider; your breasts are developing. If it hasn't happened already, underarm and pubic hair will soon appear, your periods will start, and you will have the body of a teenager.

With a teenage body comes teenage concerns and lots of questions: *What is happening to me? Am I normal? Why am I getting pimples? Will I ever fall in love?* You probably have one big additional concern if your mother, grandmother, aunt, or sister had breast cancer, namely—*Will I get breast cancer, too?*

This chapter describes the changes taking place in your body and answers basic questions about breast cancer. Other chapters give more in-depth information on cancer, its diagnosis, and its treatment. You need to take responsibility for your own health and breast care. The information in this book will help you be more responsible.

Why are my breasts growing?

Your body changes during puberty so you can become a mother someday and produce milk, the baby's first food. One of the most noticeable changes occurs in your breasts. On the outside, they grow bigger and the nipples begin to darken and stick out. On the inside, changes take place to allow the breasts to make and store milk.

Breasts, like people, come in different shapes and sizes: big or small, pointy or flat, high or low, firm or droopy. The small tip of the breast is called the *nipple*. The nipple is where the milk will come out if you have a baby. The *areola*, a circle of darker skin, surrounds the nipple.

What is inside my breast?

Each of your breasts contains fifteen to twenty *milk glands* arranged like spokes in a wheel. Fat fills the spaces surrounding them. A milk gland looks like a tiny bunch of grapes. It branches into small clusters called *lobules* where milk can be produced. Every milk gland has its own set of ducts, or tubes, that lead to the nipple. If you become a nursing mother, milk will travel through the ducts to the outside of your nipples. Breasts also consist of nerves, blood vessels, lymph vessels, and connective tissue. No muscles are found in breasts, but muscles lie beneath them in the chest.

When does breast development begin?

Girls usually begin to develop breasts when they are about ten or eleven years old. Some girls develop earlier, and some girls develop later. Many girls worry that they are maturing either too early or too late. You need not worry! Everyone's rate of development is different.

The starting age of development will not affect the ultimate size of your breasts when you finish maturing. Early starters can end up with big breasts or small, and it is the same for late starters—they, too, can wind up with big or

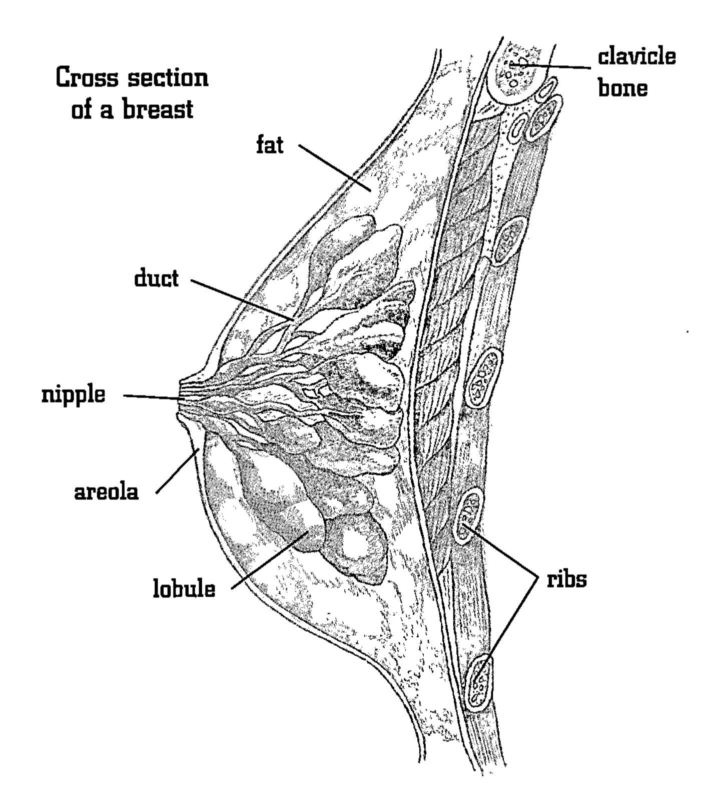

small breasts. In addition, your starting age has nothing to do with how fast your breasts will develop. Early starters can grow quickly or slowly. Likewise, the breasts of late starters can grow fast or slow.

Wouldn't it be much simpler if every girl began to develop breasts on the day she entered seventh grade and everybody finished up a year later with the same size breasts? Then no girl would have to worry about whether she was normal or not! But that's not the way it is. Breasts differ from individual to individual just like noses, eyes, and feet.

No matter when you start, your breast development goes through several stages. During childhood, breasts are flat with a slightly raised nipple. When the breasts begin to develop, the nipple and areola darken and enlarge. Small buds of breast tissue grow beneath the nipple and areola,

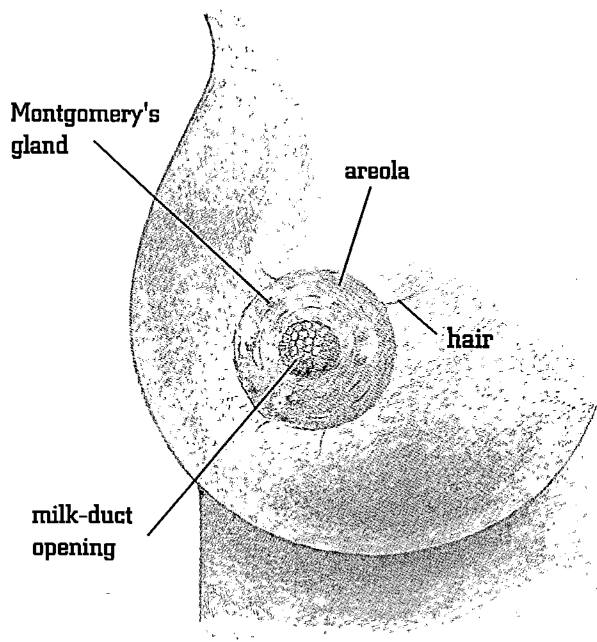

The nipple and areola

pushing them out. These buds contain milk ducts and fat. During development they can feel itchy or uncomfortable. Even though your breasts may look or feel like they are going to burst, don't worry—they won't!

In the next stage, the breast itself becomes larger and protrudes more from the chest. The nipple and areola continue to darken and grow. Then the breasts continue to enlarge. The nipple and areola may form separate bulges and stick out from the breasts, but some girls skip this stage. In the final stage, the breasts become rounder and fuller. The areola sinks back into the contour of the breast.

Lots of girls are excited about and proud of their blossoming breasts. Others are embarrassed by the changes in their body and feel more comfortable wearing bulky sweaters and oversized shirts to hide their breasts. When these girls grow older and more secure with their figures, they may switch to more form-fitting clothing.

Will exercise make my breasts bigger?

No! Chest exercises will strengthen the muscles beneath the breasts but cannot increase bust size. Your breasts consist mainly of glandular tissue and fat. Most of their roundness comes from the fat. If you are underweight and small breasted, your breasts may become fuller if you gain weight, but heredity plays the biggest role in determining breast size. Some girls who consider themselves to be flat chested may still be in the process of developing.

What do breasts have to do with sex?

Ever since you were an infant, you have known that your body can give you pleasurable feelings. It is natural to want to show affection for other people through closeness and touch. Babies and young children need lots of cuddling and physical contact with their parents. You may have gotten lots of hugs and kisses while you were growing up. When you are ready for a loving relationship with a partner, you will discover that kissing and touching can stir strong feelings of warmth and pleasure.

While expressing their love to their partners, many women enjoy having their breasts stroked and kissed. This kind of touching can make a woman ready for sexual intercourse. Some women enjoy having their breasts sucked, too. This behavior is natural and will not lead to cancer. Other women find breast stimulation unexciting or unpleasant. Nothing is wrong with them—they just respond to different stimulation.

Small or big breasts—what's the fuss?

Big or little, the size of your breasts has nothing to do with your sexuality or your ability to nurse a baby. Small breasts can give the same pleasurable feeling as big breasts when they are caressed. Small breasts can produce just as much milk as big ones.

Yet you live in a society that makes a big fuss about big busts. TV shows, movies, and advertisements with beautiful large-breasted women bombard you with the idea that bigger is better. Because of all this hype, some women with small breasts may feel unattractive. They feel they can't be alluring or desirable. For these women, padded bras and bra inserts may help them feel more attractive.

Padded bras contain a thick layer of cotton, synthetic fiber, or foam rubber in the cups. Bra inserts are breast-shaped molds that fit inside bra cups. They are kind of like shoulder pads for the chest. Padded bras and bra inserts give the appearance of having a larger bust.

Big breasts can cause distress, too. A girl with a large bust may be teased by her classmates and receive unwelcome stares and comments when she is out in public. In overweight girls, a sensible weight loss may reduce the size of the breasts. Special bras called "minimizers" can help, too. They make the breasts appear less prominent.

If you dread gym class, you are not alone. Many, many girls hate undressing in front of their classmates, and even worse, taking group showers afterward. Some girls are modest and feel uncomfortable removing their clothes in public. Others are ashamed of their bodies. If you find the locker-room routine totally humiliating, remember, there are probably lots of other girls with you who are just as self-conscious about themselves or even more so.

Do you need big breasts to be feminine?

Some people link femininity to big breasts. Being feminine, however, has little to do with breasts. It is a state of mind. Being feminine means being secure about the physical and emotional aspects of yourself that make you female. It also means accepting yourself for who you are. You can express your femininity through clothing, speech, mannerisms, and actions. No one can take away your femininity and make you feel that you are less of a girl or a woman unless you let them. With maturity, you can learn to overcome any feelings of inadequacy by accepting and appreciating the specialness of your own body. You are unique!

Can extremely big breasts be a health problem?

For some people, extremely big breasts may trigger severe backaches, breathing difficulties, and posture problems. The sheer weight of the breasts can cause bra straps to cut into the shoulders. Some women with huge breasts choose breast-reduction surgery to make their breasts smaller. Most surgeons will not perform this surgery on a young woman until she has finished developing completely.

Do women with big breasts have a greater chance of getting breast cancer?

No! Breast size alone has no connection to breast cancer.

Is something wrong if one breast is bigger than the other?

Most women have slightly unequal breasts, just as they have slightly unequal feet. The difference is barely visible. However, in many people, one breast may be noticeably larger than the other. If you are lopsided, don't worry about it! The problem may correct itself within a year or two since breasts grow at different rates.

What are stretch marks?

Stretch marks are reddish streaks that can appear on the skin when you gain or lose weight quickly. They occur when the elastic fibers of the skin lose their resilience. Some girls develop them on their breasts during rapid breast growth. Although they are permanent, stretch marks may lighten and become less visible. They are harmless.

Is it normal to have hair grow around the nipple?

Lots of women grow hair around their nipples. If nipple hair bothers you, you can shave it, pluck it, or even use electrolysis to get rid of it. Pulling out nipple hair will not cause cancer.

Why does the shape of the nipple and areola change?

The nipples and areolas may lie almost flat in a relaxed state. But they may pucker up and stiffen when you are cold, during sexual stimulation, when they rub against clothing, and in breast-feeding. This stiffening occurs when tiny muscle fibers in the areola contract.

What are inverted nipples?

Nipples that pucker inward instead of sticking outward are called *inverted nipples*. They are caused by tissue inside the breast that holds the nipple down. This condition is usually

An inverted nipple

present at birth but may not be noticeable until later. It can occur in one or both breasts. Nursing with inverted nipples may be difficult, but sometimes inverted nipples turn outward during breast development or pregnancy. A normal nipple that suddenly becomes inverted later in life (or an inverted nipple that suddenly sticks out) can signal the growth of an underlying tumor and should be checked by a doctor or nurse.

Should I worry about a discharge from my nipple?

Most women secrete a small amount of fluid through their nipples. Usually so little fluid is produced that the discharge isn't noticeable. Some girls and women, however, can produce a visible discharge when they squeeze their nipples. The fluid may come in a variety of colors—white, gray, green, or yellow. Women who take birth-control pills may find that their discharge increases.

Most nipple discharge in teenagers is absolutely normal. However, in rare cases it can indicate a problem. Infections can create a discharge with pus. Warty growths in the lining of a milk duct can cause a bloody discharge. So can pregnancy. Precancerous growths (abnormal-looking cells) and, even more rarely, cancer itself can cause an unusual discharge. Most likely any discharge you have will be normal. However, if you have any questions, do not hesitate to discuss them with your nurse or physician.

Do I have to wear a bra?

Wearing a bra is a personal decision that is entirely up to you. There is no medical reason to wear one, although there may be social pressure to use one or avoid one. Many girls and women with small or firm breasts may not bother with bras. If you are large breasted or if you engage in athletic activities, you may find it more comfortable to wear one. Bras with an underwire sewn in the base of the cups provide extra support. Athletic bras hold the breasts close to the chest to keep them from jiggling. Bras will not prevent sagging as you age.

Why do some people use slang words to refer to breasts?

Sometimes talking about breasts can be uncomfortable. Using the proper scientific name makes some people nervous because the word can carry strong emotional feelings. They may be embarrassed to say the word breast, or they may think it is a "dirty" word. Others may consider the breasts so private that they should not be talked about.

Some of the slang words for breasts are boobs, jugs, tits, knockers, headlights, honkers, hooters, milkers, bosooms, and melons. These words are often used by boys and men in a joking way, but they can be hurtful, especially if used in an offensive way. Many women refer to their breasts with less highly charged words such as bust, chest, or bosom.

What can I do about boys who make comments about my breasts?

Many girls feel embarrassed or humiliated when boys stare or make comments about their breasts. In our culture many boys and men think nothing of taunting females. Often they find it amusing to use offensive slang in referring to a woman's breasts. Sadly, almost every woman and teenage girl in our society will experience some kind of verbal harassment about her anatomy.

Some girls feel flattered when boys or men whistle or make comments about their bodies. Many others find the attention demeaning and often frightening, especially when groups of boys or men yell out as they walk by.

It is dangerous for you to confront a stranger who harasses you, but you can try to make changes in your school. Perhaps you and your friends can ask a sympathetic teacher, principal, or guidance counselor to deal with problem boys and address the issue of harassment on a school-wide basis or in health or life-skills classes. Try not to take this kind of harassment to heart. It is an act of ignorance or hostility that shows contempt and lack of respect for all girls and women, not necessarily for you personally. By taking group action, you may be able to change the environment in your school or where you work.

What is a period?

You were born with two *ovaries*, small organs in the abdomen that contain thousands of undeveloped egg cells. The ovaries are inactive until puberty begins and the eggs start to develop. This usually occurs between the ages of nine and fifteen—sometimes earlier, sometimes later. Each month, one or the other ovary produces and releases a mature egg. The egg travels down the *fallopian tubes* toward the *uterus*. If it is fertilized by a sperm cell from a man, the fertilized egg will attach itself to the uterus and develop into a baby. Most of the time, the egg doesn't meet with a sperm, and it simply breaks apart.

During the days before the egg's release, the uterus prepares for a fertilized egg. It creates a nourishing, blood-filled lining, the perfect environment for a developing baby to grow. If the egg isn't fertilized, the blood-filled lining is not needed. The body discards the lining along with the unfertilized egg. The blood passes through the vagina and out of the body. This discharge is called *menstruation* and lasts a few days to a week. Many women refer to it as "having their period." After it stops, the uterus builds up a new lining, and a new egg is released. The entire cycle takes about a month. If that egg is not fertilized, the new lining will break down, and another period will occur.

The first period is called *menarche*. It may take more than a year or two for periods to become regular. The men-

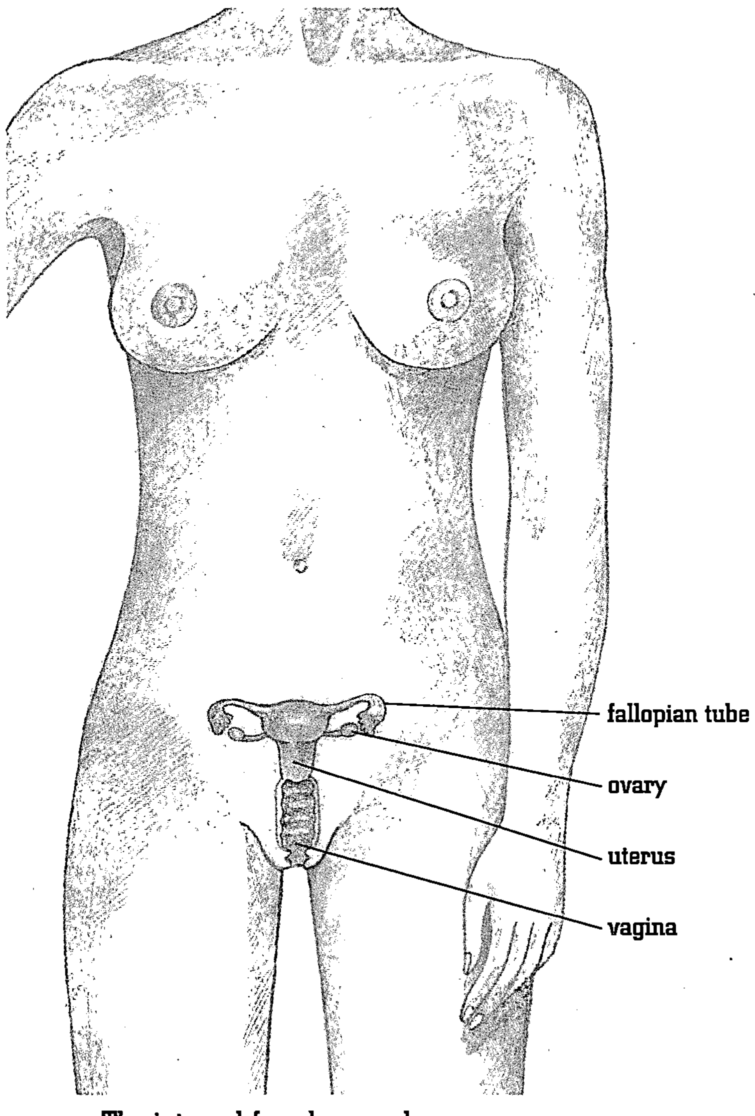

The internal female sexual organs

strual cycle repeats itself for many years but does not last forever. Between the ages of forty-five and fifty-five women go through a process called *menopause*, or "change of life." They stop producing eggs and having periods.

What are hormones and what part do they play?

Each stage in your menstrual cycle is controlled by *hormones*—special chemicals made by glands. The subject of hormones is very complicated—your body makes many different kinds, including the two main female sex hormones, *estrogen* and *progesterone*. These two hormones are manufactured in the ovaries and released into the bloodstream. They then travel to other parts of the body.

Progesterone readies the uterus to receive the fertilized egg. It also helps prepare the breasts to make milk. Estrogen causes many of the changes you see as you develop into a woman, including the growth of breasts, the appearance of underarm and pubic hair, and the rounding of your hips, thighs, and buttocks.

Why do my breasts change each month before I get my period?

Hormonal changes during the week before your period may cause a little swelling and tenderness in your breasts. Your breasts may be lumpier than at other times of the month. Hormonal changes may also cause other physical changes such as pimples, a bloated feeling, or temporary weight gain, and they may also affect your mood. Some girls become irritable or depressed. These physical and emotional changes are referred to as *PMS*, or *premenstrual syndrome*. Even before you get your period for the first time, you may experience hormonal changes and mood swings.

Will my breasts change during pregnancy?

Your breasts will begin to change soon after you become pregnant. For some women, sore breasts or nipples may be the first sign that they are pregnant. Your breasts will grow bigger and become firmer. The areola will darken, and the nipples will become larger and more erect. After the baby is born, your breasts will begin to produce milk. This takes about three to five days. In the meantime your breasts will make *colostrum,* a liquid filled with antibodies to help the baby fight infections.

What happens to breasts when a baby nurses?

When a baby nurses, it sucks some milk out of the breast into its mouth. This sucking stimulates the breast to speed the flow of milk to the nipple. The mother experiences a tingling sensation, and the milk flows out. Sucking also sends a message to the mother's body to make more milk. So the more the baby nurses, the more milk the breasts produce.

When the baby moves on to solid foods and gradually stops nursing, the mother's milk supply will diminish and eventually disappear. This process is called *weaning.*

Why do my breasts scare me?

Many girls feel that the changes in their bodies signal an unwelcome change in their lives. They are unsure about leaving their childhood. They are worried about growing up and taking on the responsibilities of adulthood. But the maturing process doesn't happen overnight. You have all of your adolescent years to adjust to your changing body and your emerging adulthood. Adolescence has many ups and downs.

When your body first started to develop breasts, you realized that you were becoming a woman like your mother. All girls think they will be like their mothers in some ways when they grow up. This can be scary to think about if your mother had breast cancer.

Many girls with a family history of breast cancer fear their own breasts. When they touch their chests, every bone and every bump can feel like a lump of cancer. These girls may connect becoming a woman with losing a breast, or becoming ill and dying of cancer. Breast cancer is rare before the age of twenty-five, so it is very unlikely that you will get breast cancer as a teenager. Don't let yourself worry! Talk to your nurse or doctor if anything about your breasts concerns you. Unusual breast lumps should be evaluated in women of any age.

Should I worry about breast pain?

Sometimes one or both of your breasts may feel tender or sore. This is a normal part of becoming a woman. Slight swelling and tenderness in your breast may be caused by hormonal changes during the week before your period. If you keep track of your periods on a calendar, you can tell if these hormonal changes are the cause of your breast pain. Simply count three weeks past the beginning of your last period.

Some teenage girls (and boys) develop a painful "adolescent nodule" beneath the nipple. These lumps are harmless and usually disappear in a short time. (In contrast, cancerous lumps are usually not painful.)

Sore, lumpy breasts can create needless alarm among teenage girls, although the vast majority of lumps are harmless. Some lumps come and go depending on the stage of the menstrual cycle. However, they can be a very scary experience if you are worried about breast cancer. To put your mind at ease about any unusual lumps, you may want to ask your nurse or doctor about it.

If my mother had breast cancer, will I get it, too?

This is probably one of the scariest questions you will ever ask, but you are not alone. Every daughter of a breast-cancer patient worries about the same thing. The answer is scary, too: If your mother had breast cancer, then you have a slightly greater chance of getting it when you reach adulthood than the average woman.

Behind your question, "Will I get breast cancer?" is another: "If I get breast cancer will I die from it?" Early breast cancer can be cured, but the outlook becomes less favorable when the cancer is quite advanced. Women have an excellent chance of beating breast cancer if they take charge of their health. As you read this book, you will learn about the many things you can do to reduce your risk of dying from breast cancer. Breast-cancer prevention and detection are discussed in Chapter Four.

What *Is* Cancer, Anyway?

The word *cancer* is a frightening one, especially if someone you love has it. Cancer is even more scary if you think you will get it, too. This chapter will help you understand what cancer is. Perhaps once you finish reading, you will find cancer a little less menacing. However, if you find this chapter too technical you can skip it for now and go on to another one. You can always come back to it later.

What does cancer have to do with cells?

Cancer is a disease of the cells. To grasp the mystery of cancer you need to understand how healthy cells work. You probably already know that cells are the smallest living part of your body. They come in many different shapes and sizes—some are round, some are flat. Others look like long, thin threads or buttons without holes. Most cells are too small to see without the aid of a microscope.

Your cells are bubblelike sacs containing tiny parts called *organelles*, and large molecules. A thin *cell membrane* surrounds each cell, protecting it and separating it from neighboring cells. An internal communications network enables the cell to sense and respond to changes in its environment and to interact with other cells.

How do cells get what they need?

Blood provides everything the cell needs—food, water, and oxygen. To enter, these materials must pass through the cell membrane. Carbon dioxide and other wastes pass through the cell membrane to exit. The bloodstream then carries them away.

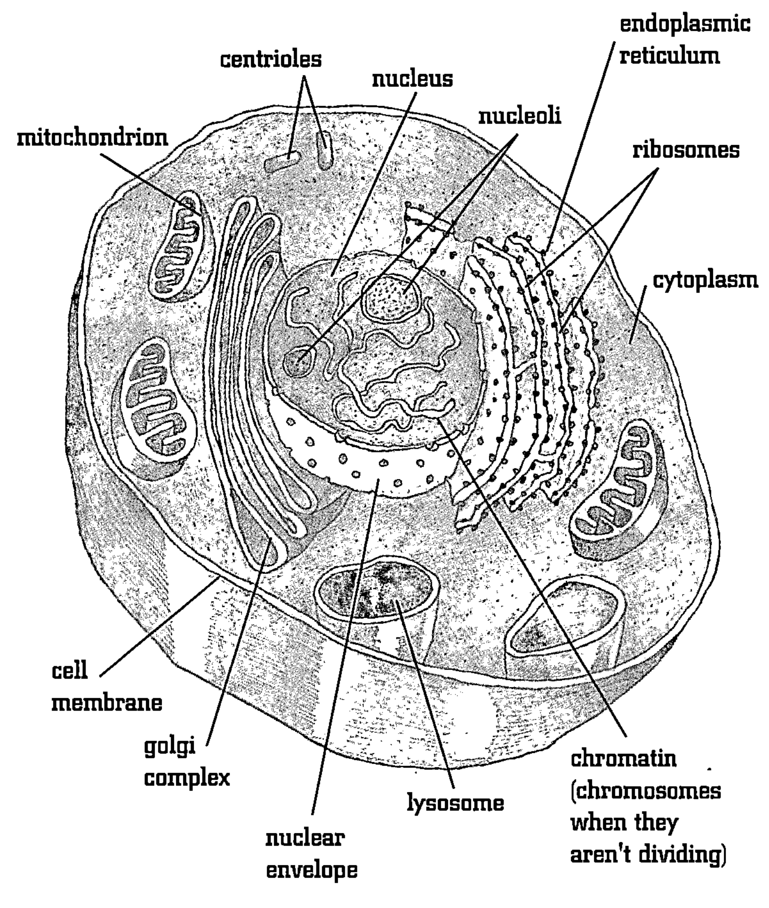

A diagram of a typical animal cell (between divisions), showing the major parts.

What do cells do?

Each kind of cell has a specific job. Skin cells cover and protect the body, nerve cells carry messages, and red blood cells transport oxygen. If you have a baby, the specialized cells in your breasts' glands will produce milk.

Cells that grow and work together form a *tissue.* In most tissues a kind of "cement" fills the spaces between cells. It binds cells to one another in the way mortar holds bricks together. Different kinds of tissue join together to form an *organ.* Your breasts are mammary glands—glandular organs designed to make milk.

How are cells controlled?

Deep inside the cell lies its control center—the *nucleus.* The power of the nucleus lies in its ability to permit the cell to reproduce. All true cells contain a nucleus. Within the nucleus are *chromosomes,* threadlike structures that contain a material called *deoxyribonucleic acid (DNA).* Chromosomes direct all the cell's activities, including growth and reproduction.

In a process called *cell division,* the chromosomes in a full-grown cell duplicate. The cell divides into two new cells with a set of chromosomes in each one. You make new cells all the time. You need them to grow and to replace damaged and worn-out cells. In some parts of your body, such as your skin, cell division occurs more frequently than in others.

Cells cannot live forever—they age and die—but the cells in your body vary in life span. Your red blood cells live about 120 days and are continually being replaced. Your nerve cells can last your entire lifetime.

What happens during cell division?

During cell division many changes take place in the nucleus. The chromosomes make exact copies of themselves and separate. One nucleus becomes two, and the cell

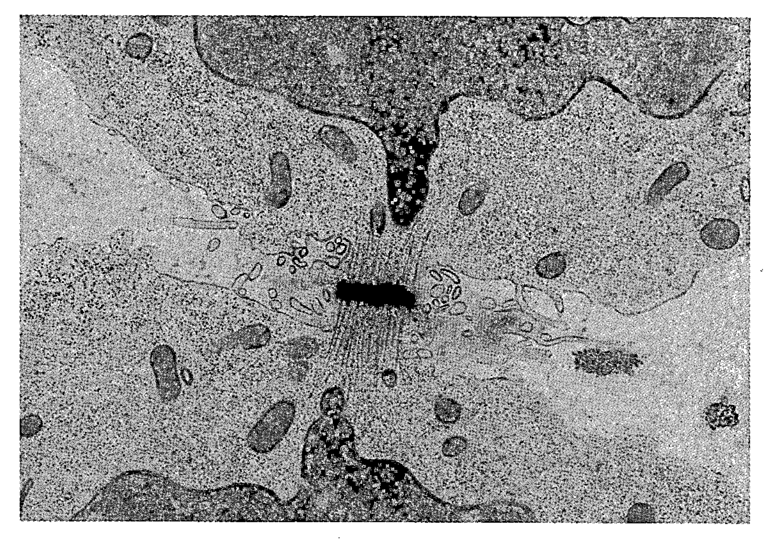

A cell that has divided

begins to pull apart. New cell membranes form when the old cell membrane breaks apart. Two identical cells now exist where once there was one. Each new cell is complete and can contribute to the health of your body. If more cells are needed, the cells can grow and divide again. When enough cells are present, the cells signal each other to stop growing. Cancer can begin when cells get the wrong signal and continue growing.

Did I really begin life as a single cell?

As hard as it is to imagine, you began life as a single cell when a sperm from your father united with an egg from your mother. Each parent contributed twenty-three chromosomes to this cell to give you a total of forty-six chromosomes. These chromosomes are the "blueprint" for you. They contain the *genes* that carry information for each of your traits. Your chromosomes hold thousands and thousands of genes, and almost all of your body cells have an identical set. Genes tell the cells how to make and shape

Your life began when a sperm from your father fertilized an egg from your mother.

each tissue and organ in your body. They even determine the color of your skin, eyes, and hair.

At first you were only one cell; then the cell divided and became two. Each of these cells divided again and again. Cell division continued until you were a ball of thousands of cells. The cells began to specialize for different tasks. Some became blood cells, others nerve cells, skin

Human chromosomes

cells, muscle cells, and so on. For this to happen, some genes in a particular kind of cell needed to work and other genes needed not to work. Scientists have found that cells contain "switches" for turning genes on and off.

What is cancer?

A cancer cell can be thought of as an outlaw. It doesn't obey the "rules" that healthy cells follow. Instead of dividing only when new cells are needed, cancer cells "go wild" and divide continually without any apparent order. They don't necessarily grow faster than normal cells; they just ignore the "stop growth" signal and keep growing. They also ignore tissue boundaries and invade neighboring tissue or even spread into distant tissue. Cancer cells tend to be less specific in their function than normal cells and cannot perform normal cell functions. What makes them so deadly is that they crowd out normal cells and interfere with many of the body's normal activities. If they block too many vital functions, then the body dies.

Cancer takes many forms. There are more than one hundred different types of cancer. They are usually named for the tissue or organ where they begin. Liver cancer starts in the liver. Bone cancer starts in the bones. Breast cancer always starts in the breast.

Why do cells become cancerous?

During cell division chromosomes make exact copies of themselves. Sometimes something goes wrong. One of the genes on a chromosome changes, or *mutates*. If the mutation occurs in a growth gene—a gene that controls cell growth—it can cause the cell to go haywire. The cell grows and divides when it is not supposed to. This change becomes permanent in the chromosomes and is passed on to each new cell.

The same result happens if the change occurs in a "turn-off" gene, a gene responsible for turning off growth

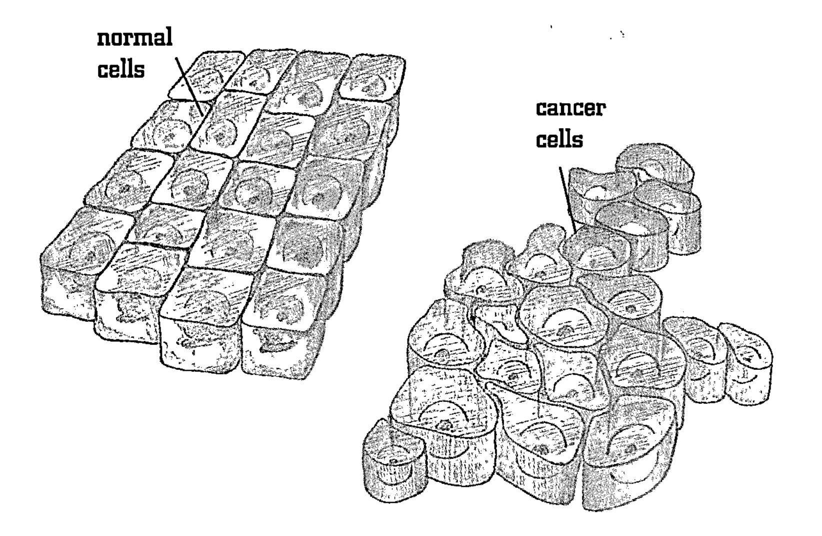

genes. Think of a mutated "turn-off" gene as a broken switch. With the "turn-off" gene disabled, the growth gene turns on. Cell growth spins out of control.

Gene mutations probably occur most frequently while a cell is dividing. Scientists think that more than one mutation is needed to turn a normal cell into a cancer cell. These mutations could occur over many years.

What is a tumor?

When cells of any kind multiply too fast without any order, they can form a lump, or *tumor.* Many people panic when they hear the word tumor. Yet most lumps or tumors are *benign.* That means they are harmless. They are not cancerous, and they do not spread to other parts of the body. Benign tumors seldom threaten life.

All tumors are caused by the abnormal growth of cells. The key difference between benign and cancerous tumors is that benign tumors limit themselves to one location in the body. Often they can be surgically removed with the expectation that they won't grow back. Cancerous tumors can spread to other tissues. If removed they may grow again in the same area.

What is a malignant tumor?

A *malignant* tumor is cancerous. It is dangerous because its cells can spread, or *metastasize*, to other tissues and organs. When a tumor metastasizes, cancer cells break off and travel though the bloodstream or lymph vessels to distant parts of the body. At the new sites they can start another tumor. That is what makes cancer cells so scary. (The role of the lymph vessels and lymph system is explained on pages 45–50.)

How can you make cancer less scary?

Because cancer can spread, it is important to find it early in its development before it sends cells to other parts of the body. Fortunately, it is possible to stop the spread of many cancers, including breast cancer, when they are found in their earliest stages.

How do noninvasive cancers differ from invasive cancers?

A *noninvasive* cancer is cancer at an early stage. It has formed a very small tumor but has not invaded surrounding tissues. Noninvasive cancers are found in one place and have only a few layers of cells. They are often called *in situ* cancers. The term *in situ* is Latin for still "in the site" where they started.

An *invasive* breast cancer, by contrast, has broken through the borders of surrounding tissue and invaded it. By the time many breast cancers are detected they have become invasive. Doctors often refer to invasive cancers as *infiltrating* cancers.

An invasive cancer is *localized* if it has remained in a single lump and has not spread to distant tissues. An invasive cancer with *regional* involvement has just begun to spread. Its cells may have metastasized to other nearby tissues, such as the skin, or they may have become trapped by lymph nodes close by. (Lymph nodes are explained on page

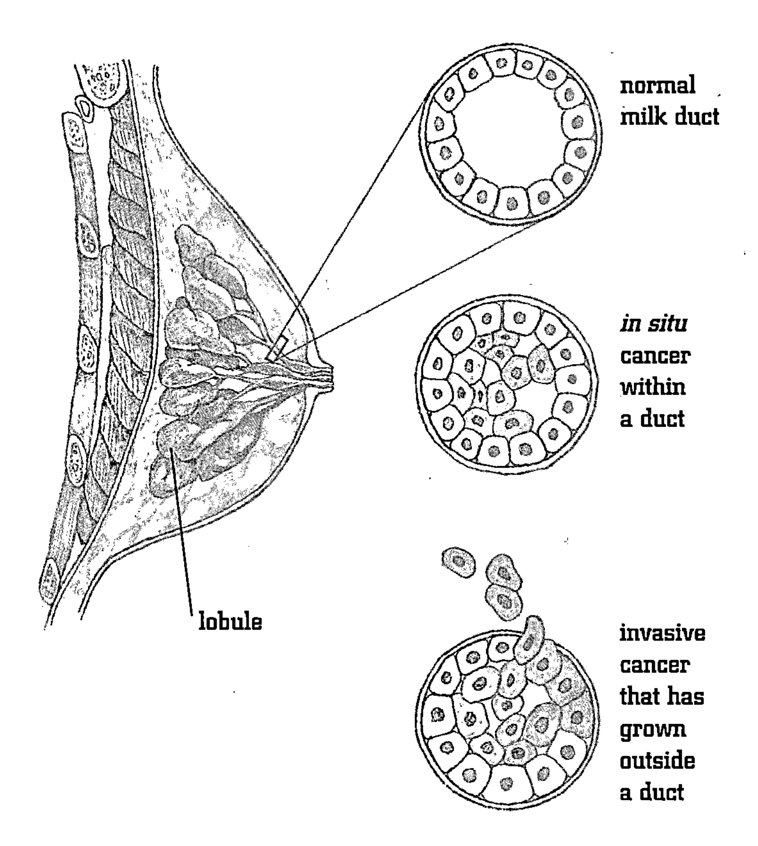

Enlarged view of a milk duct

45.) In time, invasive cancers will spread to distant sites far from the original site. A cancer cell from the breast can travel to the bones, lungs, liver, and other parts of the body.

What is the difference between primary cancer and secondary cancer?

A *primary* tumor refers to the place where cancer first develops. If the cancer spreads to more distant parts of the body, it will form *secondary* tumors. When breast cancer spreads, it is still breast cancer even if it grows in the bones, lungs, or liver.

What is breast cancer?

Breast cancer is cancer that originates in the breast. There are several different kinds of breast cancer. Almost all begin in the *epithelial* cells that line the milk ducts and milk lobules. Epithelial cells cover the inside and outside surfaces of organs. Cancers that arise in epithelial cells are called *carcinomas*.

Nearly 90 percent of all breast cancers begin in the milk ducts. Another 5 percent or so start in the lobules. (Milk ducts and lobules were explained on page 20.) The rest develop in the surrounding tissues. These include Paget's disease, a breast cancer that starts in the milk ducts in the nipple and grows out onto the nipple surface, and inflammatory breast cancer, which begins in the ducts and spreads into the lymph vessels of the skin.

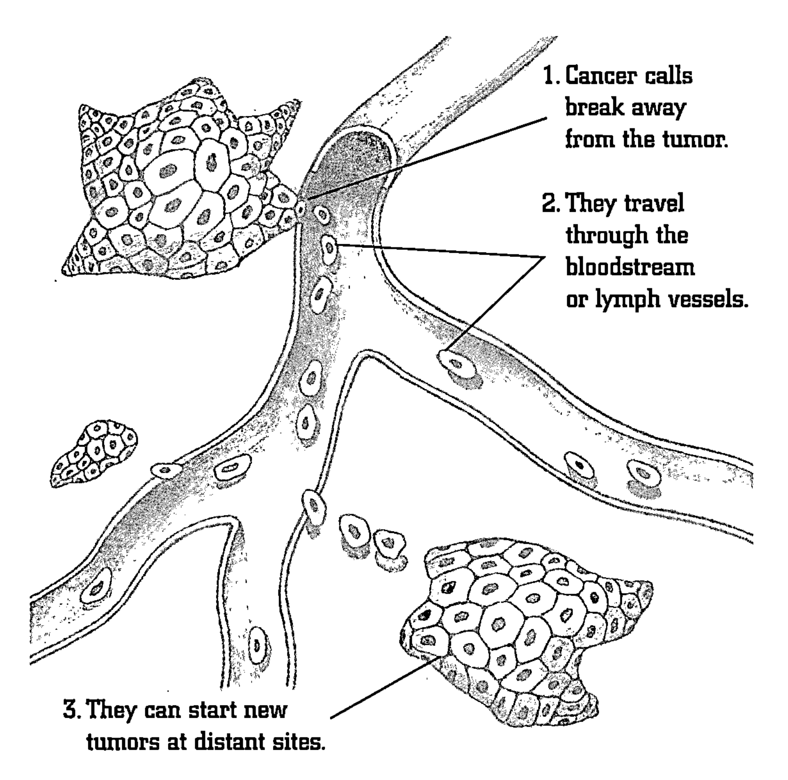

How cancer spreads

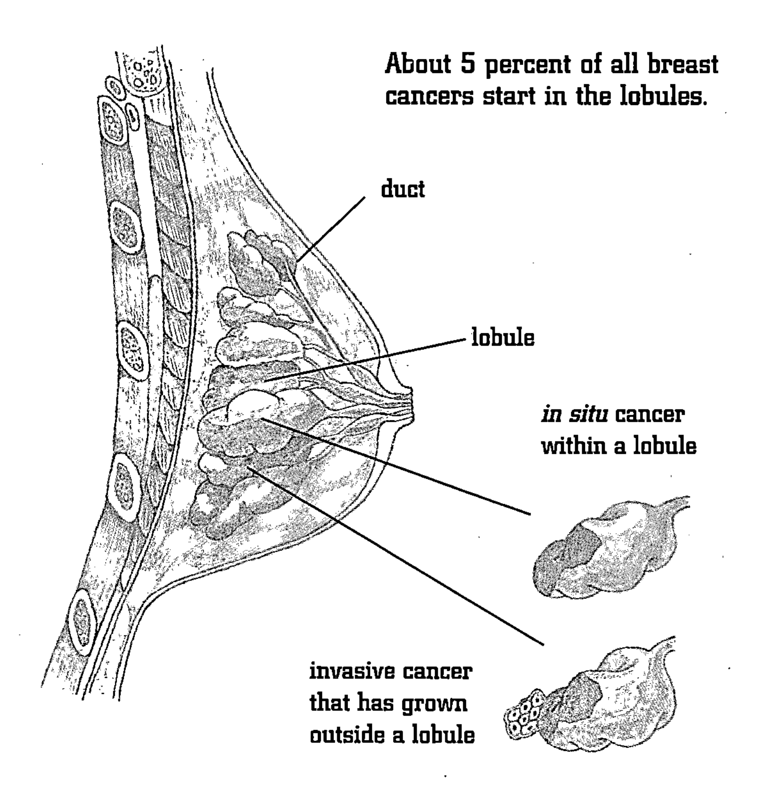

Can breast cancer start anywhere in the breast?

About 50 percent of all breast cancers form in the upper outer quarter of the breast. This area contains more milk glands than other areas. Another 20 percent of breast cancers develop around the nipple. This is where all the ducts come together. About 15 percent begin in the upper inner quarter, 11 percent in the outer lower quarter, and 6 percent in the inner lower quarter.

What are lymph nodes?

The more you learn about breast cancer the more you will hear the term *lymph nodes*. What exactly are they? Lymph nodes form part of your body's defense system against germs and other harmful substances. You have plenty of these bean-shaped structures in your neck, armpits, and groin, as well as in other parts of your body. If you have ever had swollen glands, then you have felt swelling in your lymph nodes.

If bacteria slip by your body's first line of defense—your skin—then white blood cells in the lymph system go on a seek-and-destroy mission to kill them. The lymph nodes filter out germs and poisons to prevent them from entering the bloodstream. The lymph nodes contain *lymphocytes,* a kind of white blood cell that fights infection by producing antibodies.

It may help to think of your white blood cells as cops and the lymph nodes as jails. If the bacteria—the bad guys—escape the lymph nodes and enter the blood, then your body's third line of defense springs into action. White blood cells in your blood and spleen launch a full-scale attack. The liver pitches in, too. This third line of defense amounts to calling in the army.

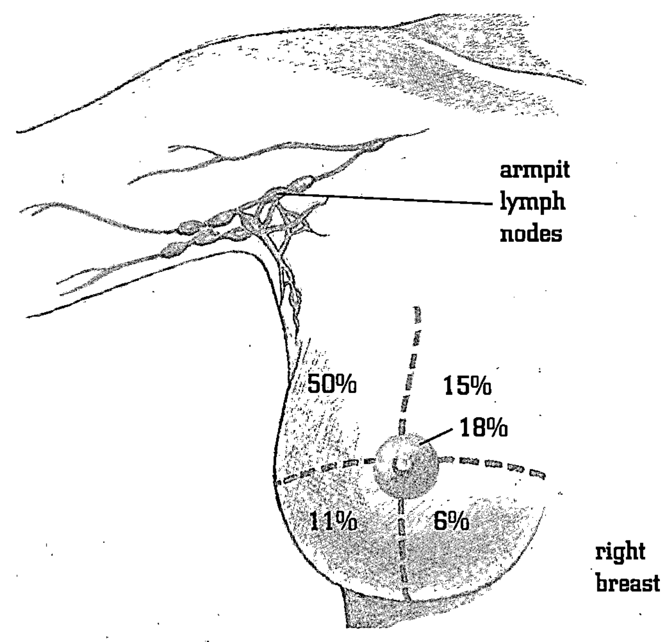

Location of most breast cancers

What is the difference between the lymph system and the bloodstream?

To really get a handle on the key role the lymph system plays in the spread of cancer, you need to know how it works. But first you need to look at how your circulatory system functions because it interacts with the lymph system. Is this beginning to sound too complicated? Stay with me. A lot of this stuff you have already learned in school.

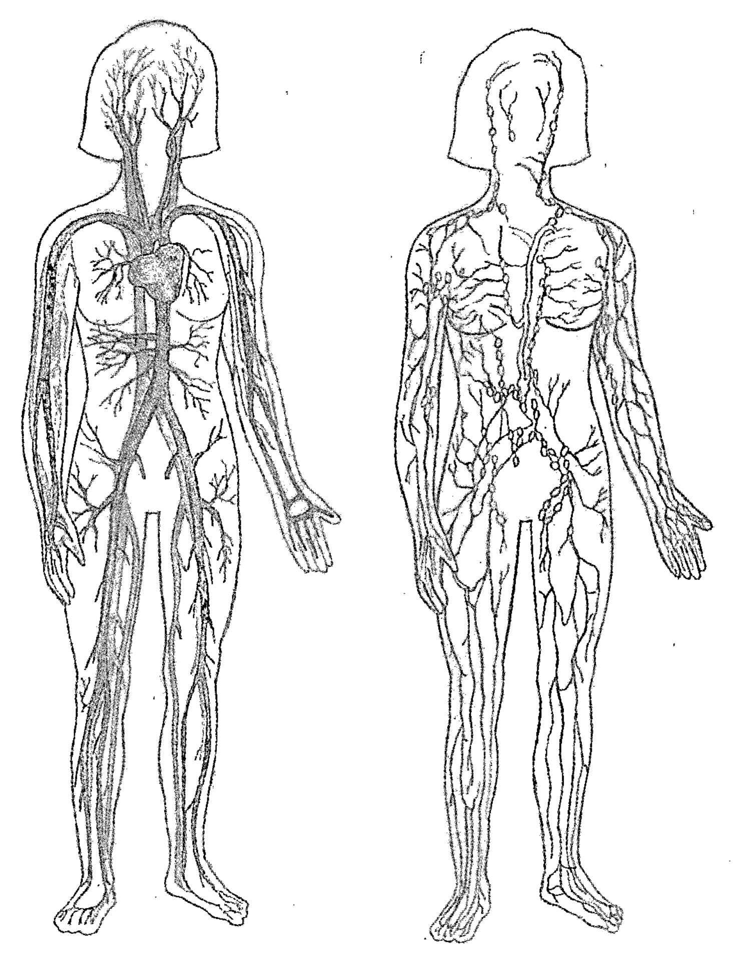

(left) The circulatory system
(right) Location of the lymph vessels

How the Circulatory and Lymph Systems Work

Circulatory System

Your heart pumps blood to every part of your body through small tubes called blood vessels. The *arteries* are blood vessels that carry oxygen-rich blood away from the heart to the tissues. They branch into smaller and smaller arteries, finally ending in *capillaries,* the smallest blood vessels. Your capillaries are so narrow that red blood cells must pass through them single file. In the capillaries important exchanges occur between the blood and the body cells. Oxygen and nutrients move through the capillary walls and into the body cells. Carbon dioxide and wastes move from the body cells into the capillaries. The blood from the capillaries then flows into *veins,* the blood vessels that return blood to your heart.

Lymph System

As blood travels through the capillaries some of the liquid part passes through the capillary wall and seeps into the spaces between the body cells. This liquid is called *lymph.* You may be familiar with lymph—it is the clear, almost colorless fluid that collects inside a blister. More lymph flows out of the capillaries than flows back in, so your body has a secondary circulatory system to return the excess lymph to the bloodstream. Without this secondary system, you would swell up.

This second network is called the lymph system. Made up of tiny tubes, it runs through your body, usually alongside your major veins, and soaks up lymph fluid. The lymph moves into tiny lymph vessels that drain into larger and larger ones. The two biggest lymph vessels empty into two veins near your heart. Lymph nodes cluster at intervals along the lymph vessels. They filter out and destroy bacteria, tumor cells, and other harmful substances picked up by the lymph.

In the breast, lymph vessels lie in the spaces between and around the milk-producing lobes. These vessels connect with lymph nodes in the underarm and lymph nodes next to the breastbone. Lymph from the breast can also drain into lymph nodes near the collarbone and at the side of the neck.

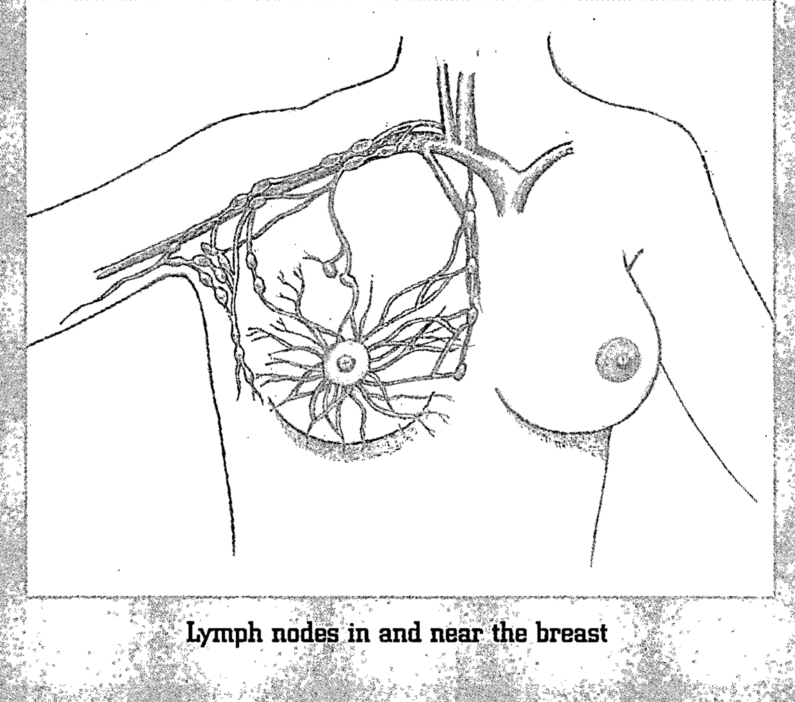

Lymph nodes in and near the breast

50 What does the lymph system have to do with the spread of cancer?

When cancer cells break away from a tumor they may be carried away by lymph fluid or by blood. The nearby lymph nodes go on the defense and filter out the cancer cells. Unfortunately, however, the nodes may become cancerous themselves.

The most important factor in determining the outlook for a breast-cancer patient is the condition of the lymph nodes. Lymph nodes that are free of cancer are called *negative nodes.* Lymph nodes with cancer are called *positive nodes.*

Positive lymph nodes are a sign that cancer cells were able to move out of the breast and get at least as far as the lymph nodes. The worry is that the cancer cells may also have gone elsewhere in the body. In general, women with negative nodes have a better chance of remaining cancer-free than women with positive nodes.

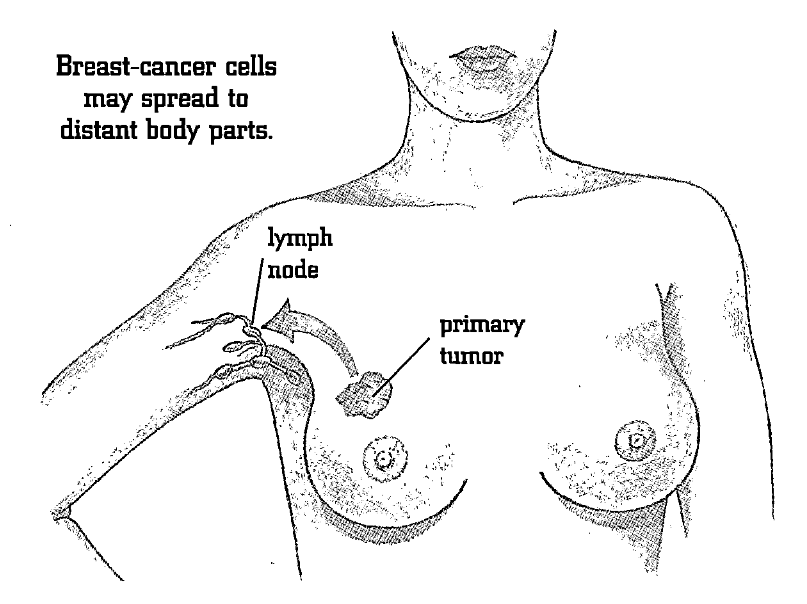

Can you catch breast cancer?

You can't "catch" breast cancer from somebody who has it, since there are no breast-cancer germs. Breast cancer occurs when something goes wrong with cells in the breast, and cell growth runs wild. It develops from cells that were once normal. Medical researchers have not been able to show that viruses cause breast cancer.

No one knows exactly what causes a normal breast cell to become a cancerous cell. It is probably not the work of any one factor, but a result of a group of at least five or six factors that interact with each other. Think of cancer as a football team—a mean and vicious football team. You can't have a team with only one player; you need lots of players who support one another. Scientists know that the "cancer team" involves chromosomes, but they haven't identified the precise role of the other "players."

Scientists have narrowed down the field of cancer-causing candidates:

- A family history of breast cancer
- The work of female hormones
- Exposure to radiation or some harmful chemicals
- Something in our diets

There is also the possibility that the cause of breast cancer is something not yet identified.

Everybody reacts differently to these cancer-causing candidates. What will trigger breast cancer in one woman will not necessarily trigger breast cancer in another. Some women are born with a damaged gene or genes and may need only a few exposures to cancer-causing agents to make cell growth go haywire. You will learn more about who is at risk in the next chapter, and how to protect yourself from breast cancer in Chapter Four.

Who Gets Breast Cancer?

You have probably heard this scary message: "Breast cancer will strike one in eight women. Those with a family history of the disease face a greater risk." Both these statements are accurate, but they don't tell the whole story. Without more explanation they feed into breast-cancer hysteria and fail to inform women that breast cancer detected at an early stage can usually be cured.

If you are frightened by the one-in-eight statistic, you are not alone. Many, many women and girls have been scared by it. They look around a crowded room and think, "One out of every eight women here will get breast cancer." And if the frightened individual has a relative with the disease, she may convince herself that she is next.

Some people mistakenly believe that the one-in-eight statistic reflects the number of women who have cancer today or who can expect to develop the disease sometime in the near future. The statistic is misleading in another way: It does not mean that at any given moment you, as a young woman, have one chance in eight of developing breast cancer. Your risk now is quite low, but it will rise as you age. Most breast cancers occur in postmenopausal women—women who no longer menstruate.

The one-in-eight odds take into account women who live to age ninety-five or older. An average woman has one chance in eight that she will develop breast cancer in the course of her lifetime. But the risk is not the same at all ages.

What are the odds at different ages?

According to statistics provided by the American Cancer Society, the odds for a woman getting breast cancer by age twenty-five is only 1 in 14,985! That means that only 1 woman out of 14,985 women will get breast cancer by the time she is twenty-five. The odds of breast cancer appearing by age thirty is 1 in 2,212; by age forty it is 1 in 235; and by age fifty the risk is 1 in 54. Most women who get breast cancer develop it after age sixty-five.

But what do all these numbers really say about your risk? The statistics may apply to you, or they may not. They underestimate the risk for women who have a mother or sister with the disease. They overestimate the risk for women with no family history. In addition, the risk factors for breast cancer may change dramatically between now and the time you enter old age. Researchers have no idea what the risks will be in the future.

No one can say for sure whether or not you will get breast cancer. Because everybody is different, doctors cannot give you an exact answer. It is ironic that medical researchers can observe that one woman in eight will get breast cancer, but they can not reliably identify the women who will get it.

Are all women at risk?

Probably every woman worries about breast cancer at some time. This shouldn't be surprising—every woman is at some risk to get it. Approximately 20 percent of all breast cancers develop in women with a family history of the disease. The other 80 percent appear in women with no known family history of it. Your risk of getting breast cancer depends on a variety of factors, which will be discussed shortly. However, even women at higher risk usually have less than a 30 percent chance of developing breast cancer themselves. That means most women with a family history of breast cancer will not get it themselves.

What causes most breast cancer?

Most breast cancers arise from mutations that take place in breast cells after birth. These mutations cannot be passed from parent to child because they did not occur in a sperm or egg cell—the cells that transmit genetic information from one generation to the next. Approximately 5 to 10 percent of breast cancers are caused by an inherited cancer-causing gene. This means most breast cancers are not triggered by an inherited gene.

Who is at higher risk to get breast cancer?

Having a mother or sister with breast cancer puts you at greater risk of getting breast cancer. So does having an aunt or grandmother with the disease, but not quite as much. The key is whether the cancer appeared before menopause. The earlier cancer appears, the more likely it is connected to hereditary factors.

The women at highest risk are those who have two or more close relatives (mother or sisters) with breast cancer.

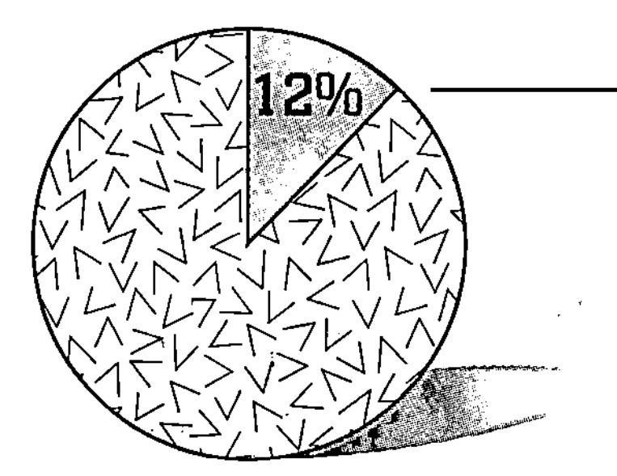

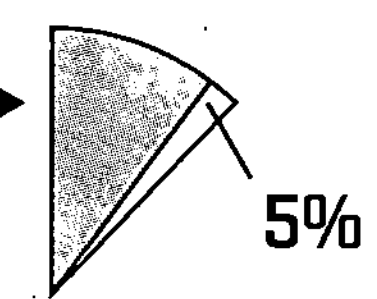

One in eight women will get breast cancer in her lifetime. Fewer than 5 percent of these cancers are due to a known inherited cancer-causing gene.

So are women whose mothers or sisters contracted the disease before menopause or had it in both breasts. These women may have a genetic *predisposition*, or tendency, to breast cancer. They may have inherited a defective gene that can trigger breast cancer.

On the other hand, the older a woman is when breast cancer arises, the less likely it is that the tendency for cancer was inherited. If the cancer occurred after menopause and affected only one breast, it may be a result of mutations in a breast cell that cannot be passed on. If you have a grandmother, aunt, or cousin who developed breast cancer after age fifty-five, you may not have an increased risk at all. Even if you have two relatives who developed breast cancer late in life, it could just be a coincidence.

What is a cancer-prone family?

Unfortunately, some women belong to cancer-prone families. In these families a striking pattern emerges. Breast cancer, as well as other kinds of cancers, appears in many different family members, often at a much younger age than in the general population. Researchers attribute the cancers to an inherited, mutated gene. They have identified several different genes that are the culprits.

Two genes, dubbed *BRCA1* and *BRCA2*, appear to be responsible for 30 to 70 percent of all inherited breast cancers. (BRCA1 and BRCA2 stand for BReast CAncer Gene 1 and BReast CAncer Gene 2). Women who carry a mutated form of the BRCA1 or BRCA2 gene have a 50 to 85 percent chance of developing breast cancer in their lifetime. They are also more susceptible to ovarian cancer (cancer of the ovaries). Researchers estimate that 1 out of every 800 women in the general population carry one of these mutated genes. Approximately 25 out of every 1,000 women of Eastern European Jewish descent are carriers.

Try not to panic if you belong to a cancer-prone family. You still have a good chance—50 percent—of not inher-

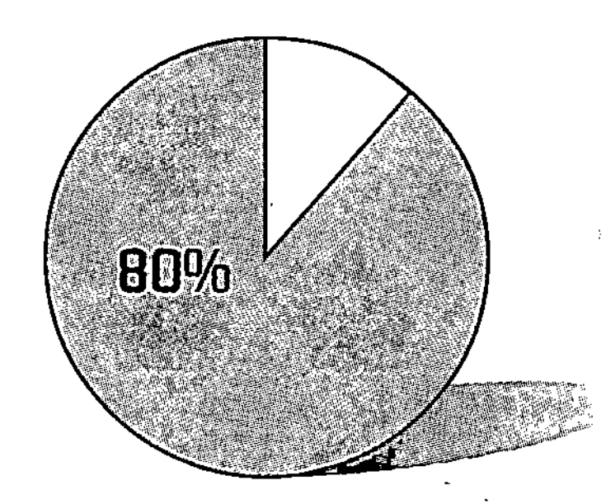

About 1 out of every 200 women carry the BRC1 gene. Of these women, as many as 80 percent will develop breast cancer by the time they are sixty-five.

iting a mutated gene. Researchers have developed a special blood test to identify carriers of the mutated BRCA1 and BRCA2 genes. The pros and cons of this test are discussed in Chapter Eight.

What happens to women identified with a mutated BRCA1 or BRCA2 gene?

Today, women who are identified with a mutated gene face a difficult choice. Should they undergo a double *mastectomy* (surgery to remove both breasts) or should they continue to live with the risk, along with careful monitoring? Removing both breasts lowers the risk of breast cancer by more than 90 percent. Yet only 15 to 20 percent of women with BRCA1 and BRCA2 mutations are choosing this option.

Increasingly, women are choosing a third option, chemoprevention—the use of drugs, to lower the risk of breast cancer. You can read more about chemoprevention in Chapter Eight.

How does a cancer-causing gene work?

Researchers believe that in families with hereditary breast cancers an inherited mutation in one gene makes a woman more likely to develop the disease. The mutation probably appears in a "turn-off" gene—a gene that normally squelches any tendency of a cell to divide wildly. The mutation destroys the gene's ability to prevent uncontrolled cell growth. This mutation can be passed from generation to generation in sperm and egg cells. How?

Remember that humans begin life as a single cell when a sperm from the father unites with an egg from the mother. Each parent contributes twenty-three chromosomes to this cell. The chromosomes contain the genes that carry information for each trait. If a gene in a sperm or an egg cell mutates, then the mutation will be passed on to the offspring. It will appear in the chromosomes of all the body cells. The offspring has one chance in two of passing on the mutated gene to the next generation. This means if your mother or father inherited a cancer-causing gene, there is one chance in two that it was passed on to you. If you inherit a cancer-causing gene, you have a fifty-fifty chance of transmitting it to each of your children.

For most traits, an individual has two genes—one from the father, one from the mother. An individual with a cancer-causing mutation from one parent will most likely inherit a normal, cancer-suppressing gene for the same trait from the other parent. For the first part of her life, the normal gene prevents cancer growth. For cancer to occur, the normal gene must mutate. The woman must acquire a mutation in one of her breast cells that knocks out or damages the normal gene. This means that even if you inherited a cancer-causing gene from your mother or father, there is a chance that you won't get cancer. In addition, you can take steps to protect yourself against cancer. The next chapter describes what you can do.

Why do inherited cancers usually turn up earlier than noninherited ones?

Inherited breast cancers usually show up earlier than *noninherited* ones because some of the necessary mutations are already present and fewer new mutations are needed to trigger the cancer. However, even carriers of a defective BRCA1 or BRCA2 gene may not have to worry about breast cancer appearing while in their teens. The cancer does not usually arise until after age twenty-five.

Is the frequency of breast cancer increasing?

Breast cancer is one of the most common cancers among women. The number of women stricken by it increased dramatically during the second half of the twentieth century. In 1940, when breast-cancer statistics were first recorded, there were about 56 cases for every 100,000 women. Between 1940 and 1982, the rate increased by about 1 percent per year. The growth rate jumped between 1982 and 1988 to 4 percent per year. By the mid-1990s, the number of breast-cancer cases was about 110 cases for every 100,000 women—nearly double the rate of 1940. An estimated 175,000 new cases of breast cancer in women were detected in 1999 in the United States.

Researchers attribute the steady rise in breast-cancer rate between 1940 and 1982 to changes in lifestyle, such as women delaying childbearing and having fewer children.

The surge in the breast-cancer rate between 1982 and 1988 is partly attributed to better detection methods. More breast cancers were discovered at an earlier stage than could have been picked up previously. If left alone, some of these very early growths—the *in situ* cancers—might never have progressed into full-fledged cancers. They might have stayed where they originated and not spread.

Another cause for the increase in breast cancer can be attributed to increased life expectancy. Women live longer today than in previous generations, so more women are around to get the disease.

The "good" news, however, is that the rate of increase in new cases has stopped rising and begun to level off. Also, the death rate from breast cancer has started to drop from a peak of 27 deaths for every 100,000 women in 1988. The decline can be accredited to the benefits of early screening and more successful treatments. Women are finding the disease earlier and living longer after it has been detected. Most don't die prematurely from it.

Still, the grim news is that more than 43,000 women a year die from breast cancer. Something must be done to bring this number down. You can help by making sure you don't become one of these statistics.

What are risk factors?

Breast cancer is a very complex disorder. It does not have a single cause, but has many causes that interact with each other over time. As you already know, in some cancer-prone families, heredity plays a major role. But what else increases the risk? Why are women today more likely to get breast cancer than in the past?

Scientists believe that genes can be damaged by exposure to cancer-causing agents in the environment. For example, cigarette smoke clearly has been shown to cause lung cancer. If you smoke, you increase your risk of getting lung cancer. Sunlight is linked to skin cancer. If you sunbathe frequently, you increase your risk for skin cancer.

You can protect yourself from lung cancer by not smoking, and from skin cancer by avoiding prolonged exposure to the sun and by using sunscreen. Protecting yourself against breast cancer, however, is not as easy. The risk factors for breast cancer are not as clear-cut except for one, and it is unavoidable.

Did you know that the greatest risk factor for you and all other girls and women is your sex? Some men get breast cancer. However, having female hormones increases the risk of breast cancer. That is why the vast majority of people with breast cancer are women, not men. It seems so unfair!

Other possible risk factors include environmental pollutants and radiation. Lifestyle choices, such as a poor diet and drinking alcohol, may also have a strong effect upon your chance of getting breast cancer.

How can female hormones be a risk factor since they occur naturally?

During each menstrual cycle, a woman experiences hormonal surges. In the first part of the cycle, estrogen rises and then falls; in the second part, progesterone peaks and then wanes. This ebb and flow of hormones stimulates the growth of breast cells.

The chromosomes of breast cells may be more vulnerable to mutation-causing agents during cell division than at other times. If a harmful chemical appears during rapid cell growth, it is more likely to damage the chromosomes, and that could lead to breast cancer later. This means that while female hormones alone are not cancer-causing agents, they are cancer-promoting agents. They set the stage for cancer to occur, and they can fuel the growth of cancer cells. Think of it this way: Female hormones are to breast cancer what fertilizer is to plants.

The longer a woman is exposed to monthly hormonal changes, the greater her risk of developing breast cancer. Women who begin menstruating before age twelve have a slightly greater chance of developing breast cancer than those who started their first periods at a later age. Don't panic if you got your period early. Remember, your risk has increased only very, very slightly. Women with a late menopause—after age fifty-five—also have a slightly increased likelihood of developing breast cancer than women with an earlier menopause. There is some suspicion that women who take additional estrogen hormones after menopause have a higher risk of breast cancer than those who do not take estrogen.

When is breast tissue most susceptible to harmful mutations?

Doctors suspect that breast tissue is especially sensitive to harmful mutations during breast development—from the beginning of puberty to the birth of a first child. Pregnancy hormones cause the breast to complete its development. They transform breast cells somehow and make them less likely to mutate. Women who have their first child after thirty, or who have never given birth, remain more vulnerable to harmful mutations for a longer period than women who have a baby while in their teens or twenties.

This may explain why women who give birth in their teens have slightly less chance of getting breast cancer later in life than women who give birth for the first time after the age of thirty. This doesn't mean you should rush to have a baby in your teens or early twenties. The slightly lower risk gained by delaying childbirth isn't significant enough to justify bearing a baby before you are ready.

Women have always had periods. What makes the difference nowadays?

Lifestyle changes that affect the reproductive system may be one of the major reasons behind the soaring breast-cancer rates during the last half of the twentieth century. In the 1940s the average age for starting menstruation was twelve to thirteen years, and the average age at which a woman had her first baby was twenty-one to twenty-two years. That meant the typical woman was exposed to monthly hormonal changes for only nine years or so before her breast cells were matured by pregnancy hormones and became less likely to mutate. Today, the average woman begins to menstruate between the ages of eleven and twelve and may delay childbearing until she is in her late twenties or thirties. Her exposure to hormone surges lasts about twenty years before her breast cells fully mature.

Family planning may also play a role in increasing breast-cancer risk. Women today give birth to fewer children than women did before the widespread use of birth control. Pregnancy and nursing interrupt the menstrual cycle and decrease exposure to fluctuating hormone levels. Many years ago, bearing five to nine children was common. The more children a women had, the less her body was exposed to hormonal changes. So how much difference does this make? If you start menstruating at age twelve, give birth to two babies later, nurse them, and stop menstruating at age fifty-one, you will have more than four hundred periods. Compare this with your female ancestors who lived one hundred years ago. Most likely their periods started at age fifteen or sixteen, they married in their teens, and they gave birth to many children and nursed them. Your ancestors may have had only a small fraction of the periods that you can expect to have in your lifetime.

Don't let all these statistics on periods and estrogen make you fearful of your own hormones. About 60 or 70 percent of all breast cancers cannot be explained by estrogen and other known risk factors. Besides, living in the "good old days" wasn't that healthy. The average person didn't live as long then as the average person does now. For example, in 1920, the life expectancy for a baby girl was about fifty-four years. The life expectancy for a baby girl born in 2000 is almost eighty years.

Does "the pill" cause cancer?

To avoid unwanted pregnancy, millions of women in industrialized societies such as the United States use some form of birth control during *sexual intercourse*. Many of these women take birth-control pills to prevent *ovulation*—the release of an egg every month. (If no egg is released, there can be no baby even if a woman has sex.) Different varieties of "the pill" exist, and the way they work is quite complicated. Most contain both estrogen and progesterone, the hormones that control the female reproductive cycle.

The pill is easy to use. A woman takes a hormone-containing pill every day for twenty-one days to block ovulation. For the next seven days she takes no pills (or she takes dummy pills that have no hormones in them). This makes her hormone levels fall and her period begin. Then she starts the pill cycle again. *A word of caution about the pill: While it does prevent pregnancy, it does not stop the spread of AIDS or other sexually transmitted diseases.*

Several studies have explored a possible connection between the pill and breast cancer. In the late 1960s and early 1970s when the pill was first widely used, it contained much higher amounts of estrogen and progesterone than it does today. Women who used it between the ages of twenty and thirty increased their risk of getting breast cancer. These women are now in their late forties and fifties.

Today, the pill uses much lower hormone doses than the earlier version. Most studies suggest that the pill now poses little breast-cancer risk to most women, and that the pill decreases the chance of ovarian cancer. However, some studies suggest a small increased breast-cancer risk among women who began taking the pill at a young age, and among long-term users of the pill. When the time comes for you to think about birth control, you will need to discuss the options with your nurse or physician.

Is there a link between a high-fat diet and breast cancer?

American women are five times more likely to get breast cancer than women in China and Japan. However, Chinese and Japanese women who move to America increase their likelihood of getting breast cancer. Their American-born daughters face an even greater risk than their mothers.

In the 1980s scientists sought an explanation. A high-fat diet seemed to be a likely suspect because the American diet is laced with things like fatty meats, french fries, and ice cream, and the typical Asian diet is not. Yet, in a major study of the eating habits of nearly 90,000 American nurses, researchers could not find evidence that linked breast cancer to adult women with high-fat diets.

This study didn't investigate the impact of a truly low-fat diet on breast-cancer prevention. A high-fat diet in adult women may not contribute to their breast-cancer risk, but it certainly isn't doing anything to decrease it. Perhaps a truly low-fat diet may help in preventing breast cancer. This needs to be investigated by scientists.

Don't use the findings of the nurses' study as an excuse to eat a lot of fatty foods. It is possible that a high-fat diet during adolescence may increase breast-cancer risk. After all, your teenage years are the time when breast tissue grows most rapidly.

Researchers have begun to study the possibility of a link between breast cancer and a teenage diet high in fat. Their findings won't do you much good, however. They'll come out about the time you have teenage daughters or even granddaughters!

Do overweight women face a greater breast cancer risk?

Before menopause, obese women actually have a slightly lower risk of developing breast cancer than others because they tend to get their periods less frequently. They have lower estrogen levels than average, and this probably puts them at less risk.

This is not a reason to overeat and pack on weight. After menopause, overweight women have a slightly higher risk of developing breast cancer. Body fat produces estrogen, so even after the ovaries shut down for good, obese women still have some estrogen circulating in their bodies.

Do all groups of women face the same risk?

All women worldwide are at risk to get breast cancer, but it is more common in women from North America and Northern Europe, and in women who rank above average in income and education. Within the United States, native Hawaiian women, women of European-Jewish descent, and women of Norwegian and Swedish heritage face an increased risk. Native American women and women of Chinese, Japanese, Filipino, or Mexican descent have a lower risk than white women.

African-American women are more likely than white women to get breast cancer before age forty-five, and less likely to get it after forty-five. These women also have a greater chance of dying from breast cancer if they develop it. The higher death rate may be due in part to inferior health care among poor African-American women. African-American women may also face a more aggressive form of the disease.

Don't have a panic attack if you fall into one of these groups! Your risk is only slightly increased, and the next chapter tells you how you can protect yourself.

Is breast cancer more common in some parts of the United States than in others?

Yes. The regions in the United States with the highest rate of breast-cancer cases are the San Francisco Bay area, the Northeast, and Mid-Atlantic regions. Some researchers suspect that environmental factors may be responsible, and they are investigating areas where breast-cancer cases are higher than average. Interestingly, one study of a population in the Northeast showed that most of the increased breast-cancer risk could be explained by lifestyle choices—such as having a first child later in life and using hormones after menopause—and by other known nonenvironmental risk factors.

How does radiation trigger cancer?

Radiation can damage chromosomes by mutating genes or rearranging them. Diagnostic X rays are probably the most likely source of radiation exposure for you. The amount of radiation you receive from a single medical X ray is quite small and probably not dangerous in itself. However, women who have radiation therapy for other cancers such as Hodgkin's disease face an increased risk of getting breast cancer because they receive at least 100,000 times more radiation during the course of their therapy than they would receive in a normal chest X ray. It takes a long time—sometimes twenty or more years—for cancer caused by radiation to appear.

Is our environment hazardous?

Since the majority of breast cancers cannot be explained by estrogen and other known risk factors, researchers are trying to pinpoint other triggers. Many scientists believe that toxins (poisons) in the environment may play a significant role in the soaring breast-cancer rate. Some toxins are harmful chemicals whose effects on chromosomes are similar to those of radiation—they can mutate and rearrange genes. Others encourage the growth of tumors. Like radiation, the effects of toxins often show up decades after exposure.

One suspect is *DDT*, a banned pesticide. DDT came into widespread use after World War II to combat insects. It acts like estrogen and encourages rapid cell growth. DDT may pose much less risk to you than to the women of your mother's generation who were exposed to it between 1945 and 1972, when it was banned in the United States. In the mid-1970s the Israeli government eliminated the use of DDT, and breast-cancer rates in Israel dropped dramatically. However, three American studies published in the late 1990s showed no connection between DDT and breast cancer. More DDT research is under way.

Another estrogen copycat under scrutiny is *dieldrin*. Dieldrin is a pesticide once commonly used to protect corn and cotton crops, and for termite control. In the late 1980s it was totally banned in the United States. A 1999 Danish study inferred a link between dieldrin and breast cancer.

What other chemicals in the environment are suspect?

Although DDT and dieldrin are no longer marketed in the United States, other pesticides may pose a breast-cancer risk. Another suspect is *atrazine*, which is among the most heavily used weed killers today. One study in lab animals linked exposure to atrazine with mammary gland tumors. Atrazine is applied to the soil, and as a result it can end up in drinking-water supplies. The safety of atrazine and other pesticides is coming under close scrutiny as scientists look for any connections between pesticides and cancer.

Scientists are currently exploring links between breast cancer and other environment hazards, including vehicle exhaust, contaminated drinking water, contaminated landfills, and PCBs (formerly used to insulate electrical components). Investigators are even looking into food packaging, plastic water containers, plastic wrap, take-out food containers and utensils, and chemicals formed in food by high-temperature cooking. Perhaps it is not one single toxic agent that is responsible for increased cancer rates, but the effect of combining so many different toxins together. In the next chapter you will learn how to reduce your exposure to suspected cancer-causing agents and promoters.

Can men get breast cancer?

Breast cancer can strike men, but it is a rare occurrence. There are about 1,300 new cases of male breast cancer per year in the United States, compared with approximately 182,800 new cases of female breast cancer. About 400 men die of breast cancer annually. Interestingly, men who carry

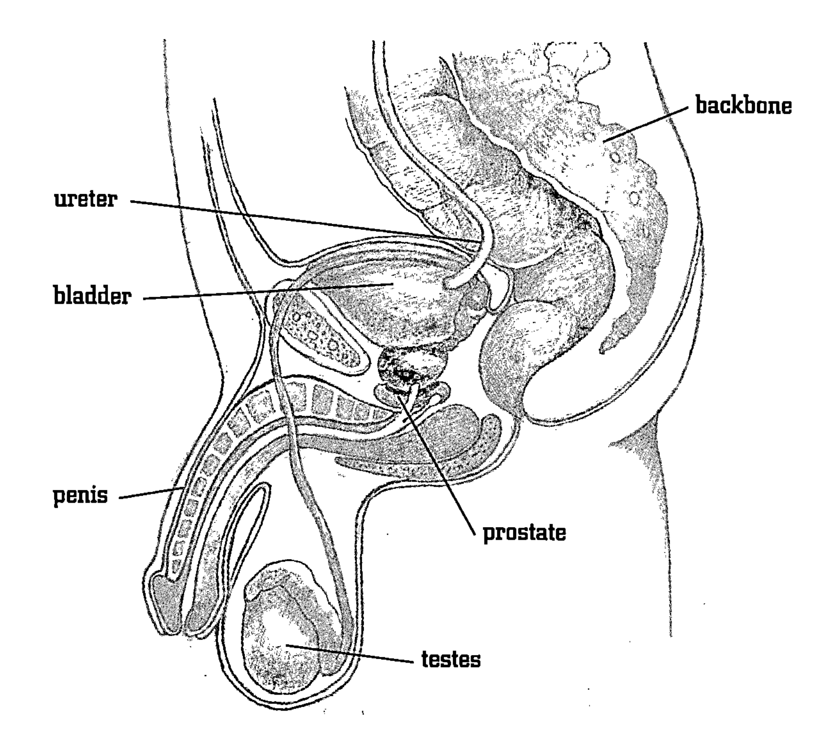

The male reproductive system

the mutated BRCA1 gene are not at increased risk to develop breast cancer. But men with a mutated BRCA2 gene are. Both groups have a higher risk for developing prostate cancer than men without the mutated genes. (The prostate is a male sex gland located near the bladder.) Men who have a family history of male breast cancer are at higher risk to get breast cancer themselves.

Will I get breast cancer if my breasts are bumped or fondled?

Breast cancer is not caused by bumping or bruising the breast. Touching or fondling the breasts does not cause breast cancer, either. Letting a boy caress or kiss your breasts will not give you breast cancer, but other good reasons exist for not engaging in this type of behavior until you are mature. The powerful feelings this behavior can evoke can lead to intercourse before you are emotionally ready.

Does wearing a bra increase your risk of breast cancer?

In their book *Dressed to Kill* (Avery Press, 1995), authors Sidney Singer and Soma Grismaijer claim that there's a link between wearing a bra and getting breast cancer. The authors interviewed 4,730 women, about half of whom had breast cancer. They found that the odds of getting breast cancer dramatically increased the longer women wore bras. The authors theorized that bras constrict the lymph system, causing toxins to build up in the breasts' lymph vessels, thus creating conditions ripe for cancer to develop.

They based their conclusions on a twelve-question survey of women's bra-wearing habits, not on thorough, in-depth clinical studies. The authors took into account the age, income bracket, and possible exposure to hazardous toxins in the workplace of the women studied. But they failed to screen for other significant cancer risks, such as being a member of a cancer-prone family, belonging to an ethnic group at higher risk for breast cancer, or being overweight. Obesity is a well-known breast-cancer risk factor in post-menopausal women, and overweight women are more likely than slender women to have large breasts and thus more likely to wear bras.

In addition, the premise that toxins build up in the breast is unfounded. The lymph nodes from the breast and chest drain under the arm and then toward the central part of the body. When drainage is interfered with, other vessels close by in the chest and shoulders take over. Bras actually facilitate lymphatic drainage out of the breasts by holding the breasts higher and applying some compression!

It is tempting to blame the use of bras for the increase of breast cancer. The solution would then be obvious—stop wearing them. But Singer and Grismaijer's study has not been backed up by scientific research.

Do antiperspirants cause breast cancer?

Medical researchers have found no link between breast cancer and *antiperspirants*. Antiperspirants reduce perspiration under the arms by using aluminum salts to plug up the sweat glands. They were first sold in the United States in 1888. Since then there has been no increase in breast-cancer rates that cannot be accounted for by the fact that women are living longer and producing fewer children. Yet in 1999 an e-mail scare campaign began. It proclaimed that "the leading cause of breast cancer is antiperspirants." The e-mail contained highly misleading information and needlessly scared many women.

How can I tell whether other e-mail warnings about breast cancer are true or not?

There are two excellent Web sites that serve as a clearinghouse for Internet hoaxes. If you get a questionable e-mail you can check it out at the Expert Guide to Urban Legends: www.urbanlegends.about.com, or at the San Fernando Valley Folklore Society's Urban Legends Reference Pages: www.snopes.com. If you can't find an answer online and you are really concerned, you can always ask your health-care provider.

For reliable online information about breast cancer, visit the Web sites listed in the Resources section starting on page 166.

What doesn't cause breast cancer?

Cancer cannot be caused by touching your breasts or letting somebody else touch, kiss, or suck them. Bumping or bruising your breasts will not cause cancer. Neither will nursing a baby.

If a pregnant woman has breast cancer, she cannot pass it onto her unborn child. If a nursing mother has breast cancer, she cannot give it to her baby through the milk. You cannot get breast cancer from thinking and worrying about it. You cannot catch it by kissing or touching somebody with it, or eating the food they prepare.

I think I am at higher risk for breast cancer. How can I stop being so scared?

Remember that all women are at risk for breast cancer, but many fail to realize it. They think breast cancer won't happen to them, so they don't take precautions. If these women develop the disease, they may detect it at such an advanced stage that it cannot easily be cured. You have an advantage. You know you will need to monitor your breasts as you grow older. If you develop the disease you will probably find it at such an early stage that it can be cured easily. Chapter Four explains how you can help yourself.

Improving Your Odds

By now (if you have read much of the first three chapters), you probably have questions of your own—like these:

- If breast cancer mainly affects older women, why do young women need to think about it?
- If the exact cause of breast cancer escapes medical researchers, how can I hope to avoid it?
- Is there anything I can do to improve my odds of preventing breast cancer?

If these and other questions gnaw at you, read on!

Experts think that the American lifestyle is partly responsible for the high rate of cancer in this country. You may be able to lower your risk of breast cancer by making healthy lifestyle choices. These choices include eating a wide variety of colorful fruits and vegetables along with a low-fat diet, exercising regularly, and steering away from alcohol. All are described in the following pages.

Does what I eat make a difference?

Wouldn't it be great to be able to blame breast cancer on American eating habits? Then you could simply avoid foods that are bad for you and eat only the good stuff. Researchers are attempting to do just that. They are seeking to identify not only the foods that may increase risk but also the foods that can protect against breast cancer. So far they have had mixed results.

Right now, the link between diet and breast cancer resembles a big jigsaw puzzle with a lot of pieces missing. As you grow older, researchers will undoubtedly discover more of the puzzle parts. Someday they will fully understand the role of diet in breast cancer. For now, the jumble of puzzle pieces presents strong clues, but no definite answers. These clues will be your guide for increasing your protection against breast cancer.

What's all the concern about fat?

Studies show that a diet high in fat may lead to higher estrogen levels in the body. You already know that estrogen sets the stage for cancer by causing breast cells to divide. So anything that elevates the level of estrogen is not good news.

Some researchers think that a high-fat diet during childhood may be the reason girls today begin to menstruate earlier than in previous generations. It may speed up sexual development and increase the level of estrogen in the bloodstream. One study in the Netherlands showed that a low-fat, high-fiber diet slowed breast development.

Why not eliminate fat totally from the diet?

Fat is an important nutrient. Your body uses it mainly for energy but also requires it in small quantities for growth and repair of damaged tissue. Fat insulates against cold and protects vital body parts from injury. To stay healthy, you must include some fat in your diet.

Are all fats the same?

Fats can be divided into two large groups. The ones that are solid at room temperature contain mainly saturated fatty acids. The fats that are liquid at room temperature contain unsaturated fatty acids. The difference lies in their chemical makeup and how they affect our health. If you are interested in science you might appreciate the chemical distinction—saturated fatty acids contain a greater amount of hydrogen atoms than unsaturated fatty acids.

Saturated fat comes mainly from animal fats, solid vegetable shortenings, margarines, and most dairy products. Try to minimize your intake of these foods. Vegetable oils such as canola, olive, flaxseed, and sunflower oils make good sources of *unsaturated fats*, which are better for you. Olive oil may be particularly good for you.

Are some fats really good for me?

Oils containing *omega-3 fatty acids* may protect against the development of breast cancer. Fatty fish such as salmon, tuna, rainbow trout, mackerel, sablefish, whitefish, her-

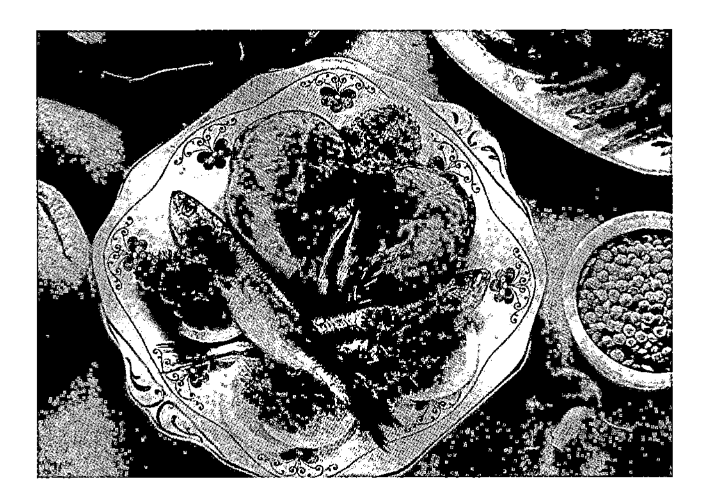

The omega-3 fatty acids found in salmon, tuna, and other fatty fish may protect against cancer.

Fat Molecules

Most molecules of fat consist of three fatty-acid molecules joined to one glycerol molecule. To picture a fat molecule, make a fist and then extend three of your fingers. Imagine the knuckles at the bottom of each of your three fingers as a skeleton of carbon atoms—the backbone of the fat molecule. This backbone is called *glycerol*.

Think of each finger as a chain of carbon atoms with hydrogen atoms attached. These fingers are the three fatty acids that make up the fat molecule. Just as your fingers are slightly different, so fatty acids vary. They can be long or short, straight or curvy. They can be filled with hydrogen atoms or have a few empty spaces. Saturated fatty acids contain all the hydrogen atoms they can hold. Unsaturated fatty acids have room for more.

Adapted with permission from an idea by Dr. Joyce A. Nettleton in *Seafood and Health* (Huntington, NY: Osprey Books, 1987), p. 23.

ring, and sardines offer an excellent source of omega-3-containing oils. Do you like to eat a lot of these fish? To obtain benefits from them, scientists recommend that you consume two to three servings a week.

Why should I worry about fats now?

As a teenager, your breasts are especially sensitive to harmful chemicals during rapid cell growth. Estrogen encourages this rapid growth, and high-fat diets increase estrogen. A truly low-fat diet with plenty of *fiber* may actually decrease the amount of estrogen in your body and protect you against breast cancer.

In the United States fat accounts for a whopping 36 percent of the daily calories for the average woman. Most of the fat comes from animals: beef, pork, lamb, poultry, eggs, and dairy products. Although the fat comes from different sources, the typical American eats the equivalent of a stick of butter a day!

In Japan, where breast-cancer rates are much lower, fat supplies only 10 to 20 percent of the calories in a typical diet. Little of it comes from meat.

Experts suggest that Americans lower the total amount of fat in their diets and try to avoid saturated fats. Here are some ways to reduce the amount of fat you eat:

- Cut down on fried and oily foods (including french fries and chips).
- Switch to skim or low-fat dairy products.
- Substitute poultry, fish, and lean meats for red meats streaked with fat.
- Remove skin from chicken and turkey before eating.
- Minimize the amount of salad dressing, butter, margarine, and rich sauces that you add to food.
- Cut down on high-fat snacks and baked goodies such as cakes and cookies.

Is it possible that fat isn't the problem?

Some researchers question whether fat deserves the blame for the rise in breast cancer. They wonder if the effects linked to fat may simply be due to a diet high in total calories. Eskimo women traditionally eat a high-fat diet and have almost no breast cancer.

Other researchers point to dieldrin and other toxic pollutants that collect in fat. People who eat a high-fat diet most likely take in greater amounts of these poisons than people who maintain a low-fat diet.

Some experts think that fiber holds the key. They believe eating more fiber—not less fat—will reduce breast-cancer risk. Fiber consists mostly of the remains of plant-cell walls. All fruits, vegetables, beans, and grains contain some fiber but our bodies cannot digest it. Its main effect is to move food and stool through the large intestine and out of the body. Some researchers think that a diet rich in fiber may protect against breast cancer by increasing the excretion (elimination) of estrogen through bowel movements.

To get the fiber you need, eat plenty of fruits and vegetables. Don't bother to peel the skins from potatoes and apples, peaches, plums, and other similar fruits. The skins contain lots of fiber. Put peas and beans on your weekly menu, and choose breads, pasta, and cereals made from bran or whole grains.

Is broccoli good for you?

Broccoli contains one chemical which breaks down estrogen in the body and other chemicals that remove cancer-causing agents from cells. Cabbage, Brussels sprouts, cauliflower, radishes, bok choy, collards, kale, turnips, and

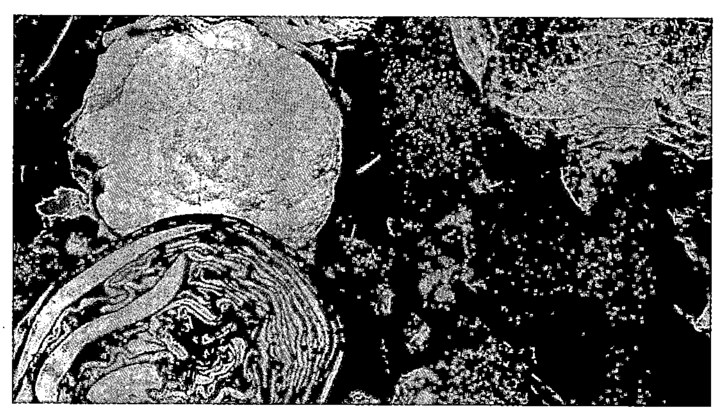

Vegetables in the cabbage family

other foods in the cabbage family also contain these chemicals. Perhaps eating foods from the cabbage family will help prevent breast cancer. Interestingly, Asian women eat large quantities of these vegetables, and they experience lower rates of breast cancer. Try to eat several servings of these foods each week.

What other foods may protect against breast cancer?

Legumes—beans, peas, soybeans, and lentils—may be particularly beneficial. These foods contain weak estrogens. Weak estrogens can bind with the estrogen *receptors* on the surface of breast cells. The receptors control the entry of estrogen into breast cells. When weak estrogens bind with the receptors, the body's own stronger estrogens are blocked from entering the cells, thus reducing the effects of estrogen.

Hispanic women traditionally eat a high-fat diet rich in beans. Yet their breast-cancer rate remains lower than that of non-Hispanic white women. Perhaps the beans hold the key. Foods containing soy may help to account for the low breast-cancer rates of Japanese women. Women in Japan consume large amounts of tofu (soybean curd) and other soy-based foods.

Flaxseed may reduce the impact of estrogen, too. Like soy, it blocks strong estrogens. Garlic, onions, and chives may hinder the action of certain cancer-causing agents. Grapes, carrots, soy, and the spices turmeric and rosemary contain a chemical that may prevent tumors from developing blood vessels needed for growth.

Researchers think that fruits and vegetables rich in Vitamin E, Vitamin C, *carotenoids*, and other colorful pigments may offer some insurance against breast cancer. These protectors go by the fancy chemical name of *antioxidants*. They fight against the toxic agents that can damage DNA. Green tea is loaded with powerful antioxidants, and black tea contains some, too.

What exactly are carotenoids?

Carotenoids are pigments found in the cells of brightly colored fruits and vegetables. *Beta-carotene* is the best known. It is a yellow pigment that helps provide the coloring for carrots, peaches, cantaloupes, sweet potatoes, and other produce. Beta-carotene does more than make fruits and vegetables look pretty. Scientists think that it safeguards against cancer.

Beta-carotene plays another important role. Your body converts it to Vitamin A, which helps your eyes detect light. You may have been told to eat carrots because they are good for your eyes. Did you think you'd ever be told to eat them because they are good for your breasts?

What other pigments may be healthful?

Tomatoes, especially vine-ripened ones, may be particularly healthy for you. They contain the red pigment *lycopene*, which may prove to be a powerful cancer inhibitor. Interestingly, lycopene is best absorbed by the body after it has been cooked and concentrated. Tomato sauce, tomato paste, and ketchup make excellent sources. Imagine thinking of ketchup as a health food?

The pigments that give plums, cherries, blueberries, and strawberries their deep, rich hue are also extremely potent antioxidants. Other powerful antioxidants are in grapes, apples, and green leafy vegetables. Lemons, oranges, and other citrus fruits also contain chemicals that may inhibit cancer growth.

Help! This is too much information to digest!

All you really need to remember is this: The more colorful a fruit or vegetable is, the greater the health benefits for you. So pile your plate high with a colorful variety of them.

New data suggest, however, that excessive levels of antioxidants may be harmful. So use moderation when taking antioxidant supplements in tablet form.

Should I rinse fruits and vegetables before eating them?

Rinsing fruits and vegetables thoroughly helps remove pesticide residues from their surfaces. Rinsing produce will also wash away potentially disease-causing microbes. So it's to your benefit to wash all fruits and vegetables before eating or cutting into them. This includes the ones with skins that will be discarded, such as cucumbers, oranges, bananas, and melons. Rinsing prevents any harmful organisms on the surface from being transferred to the edible part during slicing or peeling. Don't wash produce with soap or detergents, as these cleaning agents may leave their own residues.

How can I make healthier food choices?

By now you have probably figured out that switching to a colorful, low-fat, high-fiber diet with plenty of fish, beans, fruits, olive oil, soybeans, broccoli, and other vegetables is your best bet for reducing your odds of developing breast cancer. But the task may seem overwhelming. What is a girl to do?

The Food Guide Pyramid shown here can help. The pyramid makes it easy to choose and follow a healthy eating program. It tells you the number of servings to eat each day from the various food groups.

Making the switch to healthier eating may seem overwhelming. But the more you know about food and nutrition, the easier it will be to make the transition. Ask your librarian to recommend books on nutrition. Also see the Resources section beginning on page 166.

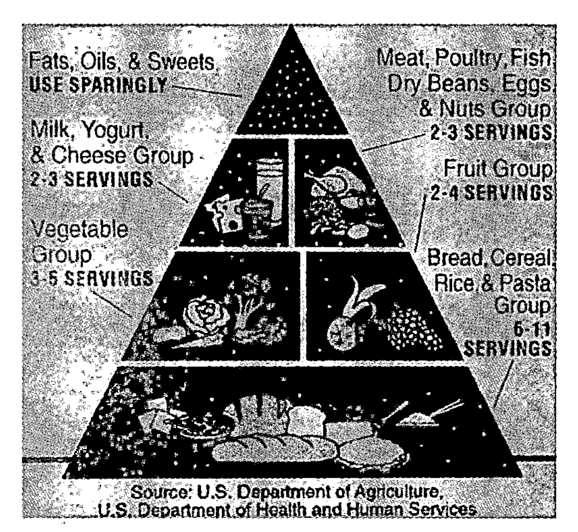

FOOD GUIDE PYRAMID
A Guide to Daily Food Choices

Why bother to eat a sensible diet if scientists haven't proven it will protect against breast cancer?

No one knows yet which foods provide the best protection against breast cancer. However, many researchers believe that it is only a matter of time before the link between diet and breast cancer will be determined. In the meantime, a healthy diet can't hurt. Eating sensibly will help you feel and perform at your peak. It will also help to protect you against other forms of cancer, heart disease, and many illnesses. Many nutritionists recommend a high-quality, well-balanced diet.

Should I join a diet support group?

If you are overweight, a diet support group such as Weight Watchers may be beneficial. These groups offer emotional support for those trying to lose weight. The leaders and other members understand about the temptation to binge on foods like potato chips or ice cream. They will share their own strategies for controlling their appetites.

These groups also give valuable advice on how to plan meals and snacks. Many of their members lose weight, but some gain it back later. The main long-term benefit of these groups is they teach you how to reduce the fat in your diet and make healthier food choices.

Will exercise help?

Women who regularly engage in vigorous exercise throughout their lives experience lower rates of breast, ovarian, and uterine cancer. To improve your odds, exercise at least three times a week for a minimum of twenty minutes. You can choose bicycling, jogging, skating, swimming, hiking, cross-country skiing, aerobic dancing, or any other vigorous exercise. Even a habit of taking brisk walks may make a difference.

You probably have been bombarded with other good reasons to exercise regularly: It strengthens the heart, lungs, and muscles; keeps joints flexible; and reduces body fat when combined with a sensible diet. Did you know exercise provides an added bonus?

It can make you feel better by reducing anxiety and depression. Perhaps you have heard of a "runner's high." It occurs during exercise when the body releases a chemical that gives a feeling of well-being. Swimmers, bicyclists, and other athletes experience this high, too.

Is there a link between alcohol and breast cancer?

Many excellent reasons exist for teenagers to avoid alcohol, and by now you probably think you have heard them all: Alcohol can harm your health and dull your performance in school. It can impair your ability to make good decisions. Drinking and driving often has tragic results. Drinking and driving a boat can end up in tragedy, too. Teenage drinking can lead to alcoholism. Mixing alcohol and other drugs can multiply the nasty effects, causing a harmful overdose, and perhaps death.

If none of these reasons have convinced you to avoid alcohol, perhaps this will: Drinking alcohol—beer, wine, or hard liquor—increases the risk of breast cancer, especially for women under thirty. The more you drink, the greater your risk.

Is there a link between cigarette smoking and breast cancer?

Women smokers have a greater chance of dying from breast cancer than nonsmokers. The more cigarettes a women smokes, the larger her risk. All people who smoke have an increased risk of lung cancer and heart disease. What does this mean for you? Don't smoke! And try to limit your exposure to secondhand smoke.

If you can't prevent breast cancer, what can you do about it?

Right now there are no foolproof methods for preventing breast cancer. However, *screening* techniques exist to find the disease at the earliest possible stage. These techniques include the breast self-exam, the clinical breast exam, and the mammogram.

What is the breast self-exam?

The *breast self-exam,* called BSE for short, is one of your keys to breast-cancer detection. It is an examination of your breasts that you do yourself. You need to become familiar with the appearance and feel of your breasts. If you haven't done a BSE before, don't be surprised to find that your breasts feel more like lumpy oatmeal than smooth jelly. The idea of the BSE is to know your breasts so well that you can detect something unusual. As a teenager the chances of your finding anything out of the ordinary is extremely low. But if you make BSE a lifetime habit, it may save your life when you are older. You should repeat the BSE once a month, about a week after your period begins. This is the time when your breasts are least likely to be swollen or tender, and are the least lumpy.

How do I perform a breast self-exam?

1. Undress from the waist up and lie flat on your back. Place a pillow under your left shoulder.

2. Raise your left arm behind your head. Use the middle three fingers of your right hand to feel your left breast. Start at the outer edge of your breast, just under the armpit. Press down firmly with the pads of your fingers—the part where the fingerprints are, not the fingertips. Make little dime-sized circles. Gradually, move the little circles around the outside of the breast in a big circle that goes up to your collarbone and then back to where you started.

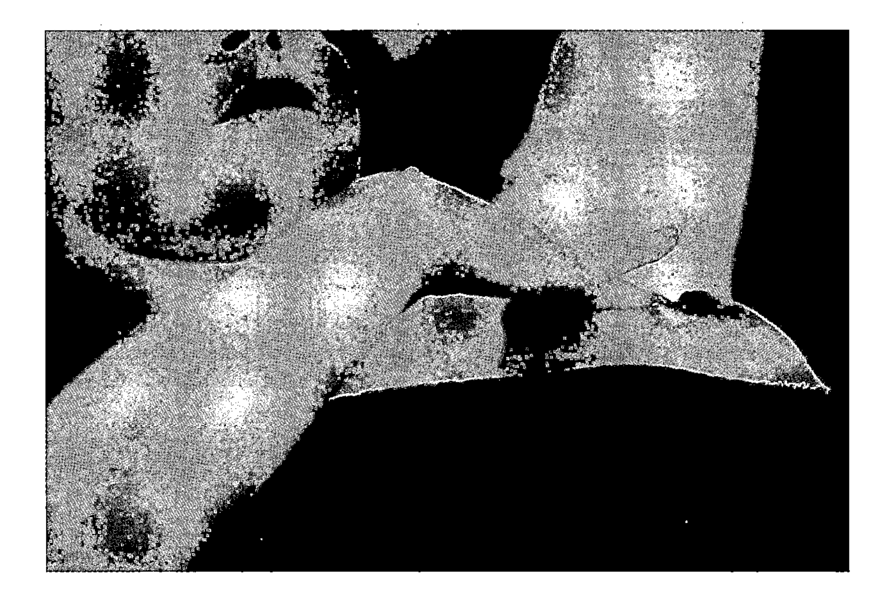

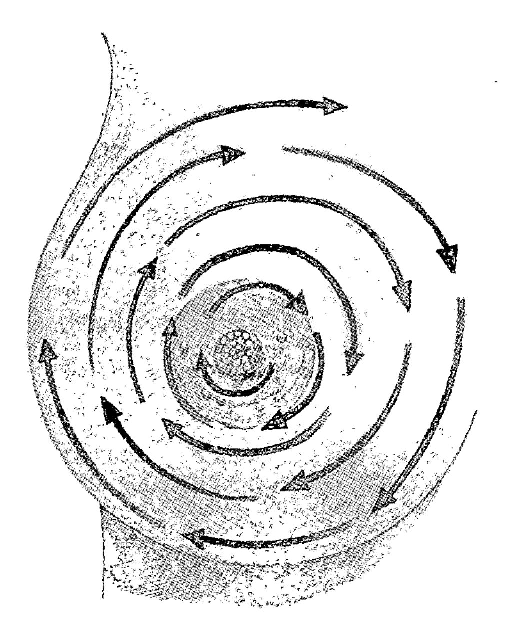

3. When you return to the beginning, move your fingers about 2 centimeters (¾ inch) in toward the nipple. Making little circles, work your way around the breast again, in a spiral. Continue until you reach the nipple. Make sure you cover all parts of the breast.
4. Then place the pillow under your right shoulder and repeat the exam on your right breast.

What am I looking for in a breast self-exam?

After you learn what your breasts feel like normally, you will be checking for a new lump or two among the usual lumps. What you are searching for is a distinct lump that feels unusual, like a piece of gravel, a marble, or a grape. If you find an unusual lump, don't panic! Most lumps found by women—young and old—are harmless. For your peace of mind report it to your nurse or doctor. You need to find out what kind of lump it is.

86 If an unusual lump isn't cancer, what is it?

Most new lumps that women find during a BSE are not cancerous or even dangerous. Four kinds of harmless lumps can be found:

1. **Cysts.** You probably have heard of *cysts*. These harmless lumps are merely fluid-filled sacs. They feel soft and round and are movable. Their size often changes with the menstrual cycle. Cysts rarely appear in teenagers or young women, but middle-aged women near menopause are prone to them.

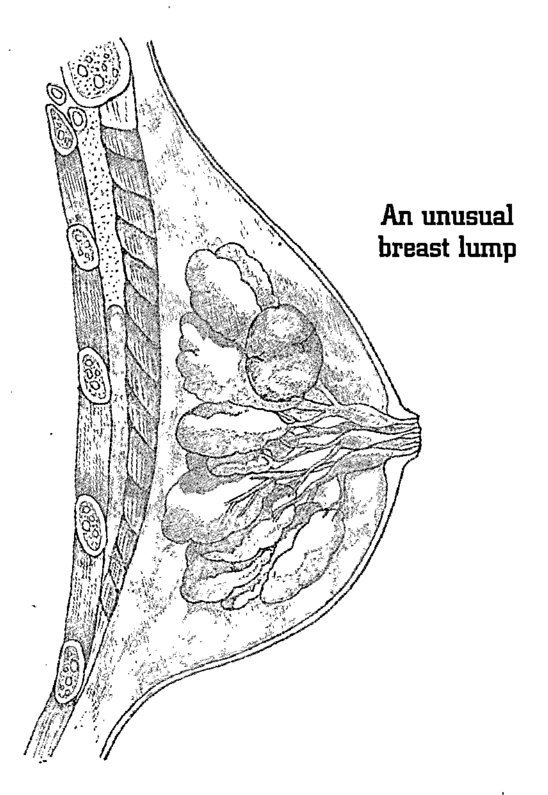

2. **Fibroadenoma.** Some smooth, round lumps have a scary-sounding name—*fibroadenoma*. They can feel rubbery, or hard like marbles. They crop up mainly in teenagers and young women. They occur more often

in black women than white women. The good news is that these solid lumps are not dangerous.

3. **Infections.** Some lumps signal an infection. For example, lumps under the armpit can be swollen lymph glands, similar to the kind you may get in your neck when you experience a sore throat. A painful red swelling in the breast of a nursing mother is a symptom of a bacterial infection of the milk ducts and glands. Antibiotics can cure it.
4. **Wartlike growths.** Wartlike growths can appear in the milk ducts near the nipple. One sign of them is bleeding from the nipple. They usually occur in women nearing menopause.

Are there other ways to check your breasts?

Some women find that the spiral pattern doesn't work well for them. They can check their breasts better by substituting a vertical pattern for the spiral in steps 2 and 3. To use a vertical pattern, imagine that you have lines drawn up

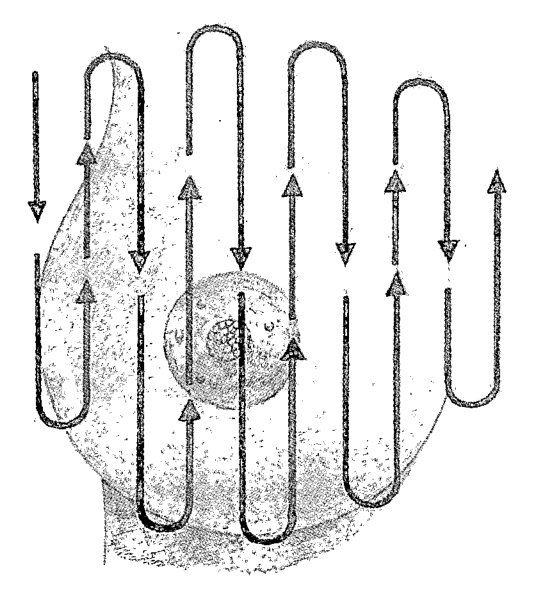

and down on your breasts, about 2 centimeters (¾ inch) apart. Beginning at your armpit, work your way straight down in small circles. At the bottom, move over 2 centimeters (¾ inch) to the next "line" and make your way back up. Repeat this until you have covered the entire breast.

There is still another technique that you can use instead of the spiral or vertical patterns. Imagine that your breast is a pie that has been divided into eight pieces. Making small circles, examine each wedge from the outer edge of the breast in toward the nipple. Go back and forth within each wedge to cover all parts of it. Then proceed to the next one. Continue until you have checked out the entire breast.

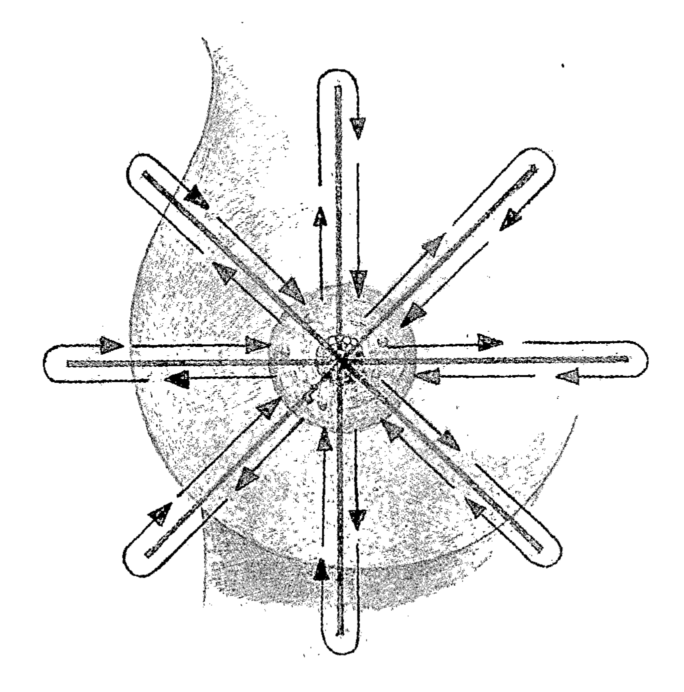

Is one technique better than the others?

No. Use the technique that best helps you check your breasts. It may take you several months to become familiar with your breasts and their normal lumpiness. What counts is that you develop the habit of regular breast self-exams.

Don't be alarmed if your breasts change during the month. Remember that the hormonal changes that control your periods also affect the breasts. They may cause a little swelling and tenderness in the breast tissue. Sometimes your breasts may feel heavier, lumpier, or more painful in one month than another. Because of the monthly variation in your breasts, it is important to perform a BSE at the same time every month in your cycle.

Can I perform a breast self-exam in the shower or tub?

You may find it easier to perform a BSE when you bathe or shower. If you make your fingers soapy, they can glide over your breast more readily. Just put your left arm behind your head and use your right hand to examine your left breast in the same way you did lying down. Remember to check both breasts.

Why am I so reluctant to do a breast self-exam?

Many girls and women feel uncomfortable touching their breasts. Some dread the BSE because they fear the discovery of a lump. Others avoid it because they mistakenly think it is the same as "playing with yourself." Most women who perform the BSE find it reassuring because they never find a cancerous lump. They feel safe when nothing unusual turns up.

The first few times you do a BSE you may feel uneasy. Breasts are naturally lumpy, and every lump may feel like a tumor to you. You may convince yourself that you have cancer! This is a normal reaction, but don't use it as an excuse to shy away from the BSE.

Right now, you don't know what is normal for your breasts. You need to learn what's "right" inside your breasts so you can tell if and when something goes wrong. The more you perform the BSE, the sooner you will find out what feels right. You will become more confident, and the BSE will become less frightening.

If performing a BSE makes you very anxious, you may find it helpful to discuss your worries with your nurse or physician. Your health-care provider will help you learn what "normal" feels like. You may feel embarrassed to do this, but your doctor or nurse will be quite familiar with these concerns about BSE, and you will probably feel much better afterward.

Why should I do a breast self-exam if the odds of a teenager getting breast cancer are very low?

Although the occurrence of breast cancer in women below the age of twenty-five is rare—1 case in 14,985 women—it can still happen. So why take chances? Breast care should be as natural a part of your life as brushing your teeth or shampooing your hair.

What is a clinical breast exam?

Another important way to detect breast cancer early is the *clinical breast exam*. A clinical breast exam is similar to the breast self-exam, only a nurse or physician performs it. Some young women (and older women too) feel uncomfortable or embarrassed to have their breasts touched by others in this way. Yet the clinical exam is very thorough and may detect lumps that you missed yourself.

Women between the ages of twenty and forty should have a clinical breast exam during their regular checkups once a year or so. Women at higher risk for breast cancer may have them done more frequently—about every six months. Since breast cancer is so rare among teenagers, most doctors don't recommend clinical breast exams for them.

Who is the best doctor or nurse to examine me?

The best doctor or nurse to check you is someone who has experience with breast cancer. This may be a primary-care physician, gynecologist, nurse practitioner, or any other nurse or physician who specializes in women's health care. If your health-care provider makes you feel uncomfortable, find one who puts you more at ease. You have the right to choose your own nurse or doctor. After all, it's your body!

What is a mammogram?

A *mammogram* is a special low-dose X ray of the breast. It gives a clear, detailed picture of breast tissue. Mammograms provide an excellent way of finding tumors too small to be felt by you or your doctor. Detecting tumors when they are small is extremely important. Mammograms can

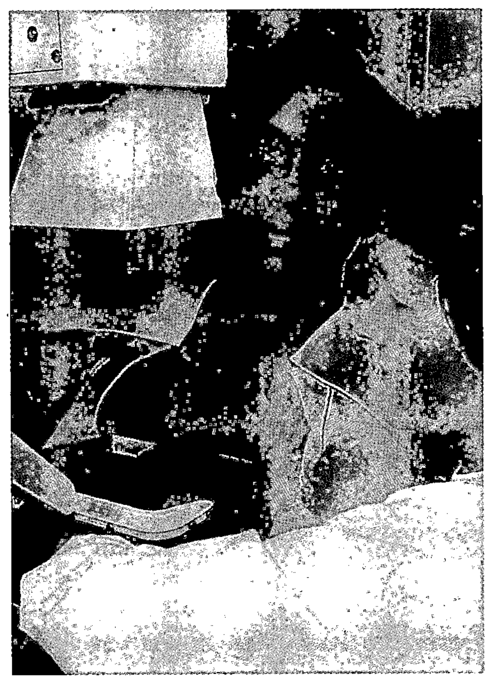

Preparing the breasts for a mammogram

also find deposits of calcium, called *microcalcifications*, which show up as white specks on the X ray. Most calcium deposits are harmless, but a cluster of them may be an early sign of breast cancer.

Breast cancer is most easily cured when discovered early. If a suspicious spot shows up on a mammogram, a biopsy must be performed to determine if it is cancerous or not. Biopsies are explained on pages 100–101.

Mammograms are not perfect. They miss about 10 percent of cancerous tumors because some cancers have the same density as the surrounding normal breast tissue. These cancers don't show up on the X ray. For this reason, mammograms don't work as well with younger women. Younger women tend to have denser breast tissue than older women. *Ultrasound* and *magnetic resonance imaging (MRI)* may be able to find tumors that mammograms fail to detect. These are explained in the next chapter.

Cancers that mammograms miss usually form lumps and can be detected during a clinical exam. Thus, mammograms, together with clinical breast exams, provide the best tools to save lives today. They will not prevent breast cancer, but they can increase the chance of finding the cancer early. The best chance of beating breast cancer is finding it early. The smaller a breast cancer is when detected, the less likely it is to spread to other parts of the body.

When should I have a mammogram?

The American Cancer Society recommends that all women between the ages of forty and forty-nine have a mammogram every one to two years. Because cancer risk rises with age, the society advises all women age fifty and older to get yearly mammograms.

The guidelines of the American Cancer Society are basically for women who do not have a family history of breast cancer. Women whose mothers or sisters developed breast cancer should go for their first mammogram at age

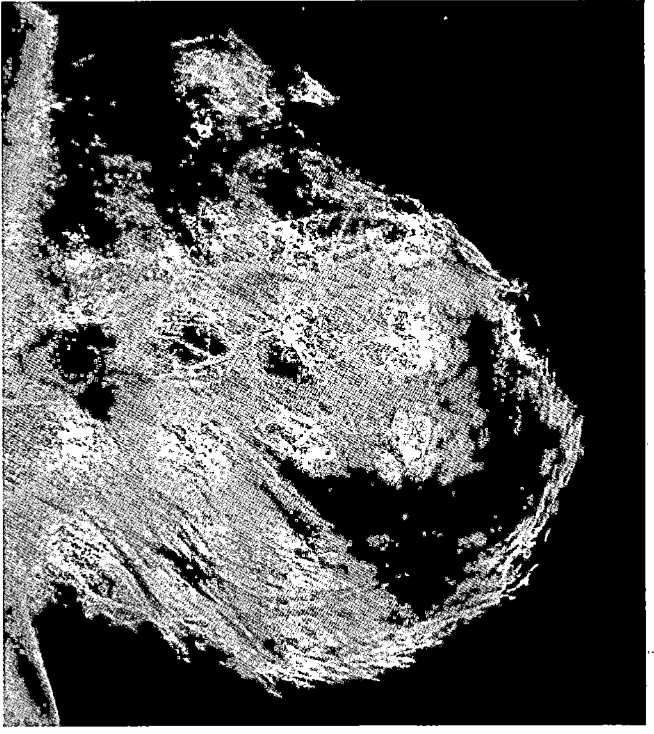

An actual mammogram showing a lump

thirty-five, or five to ten years earlier than the age at which their youngest relative discovered it—whichever is earlier. That means if your mother detected her breast cancer at age forty-four, you should have your first mammogram by age thirty-four. Check with your doctor about the best time for you to start regular mammograms. Perhaps by the time you are old enough to need one, better screening techniques will be available.

Are breast self-exams and mammograms worth the fuss?

- The average lump revealed by regular yearly or biyearly mammograms is 3 millimeters (⅛ inch). Lumps this size can't be picked up by breast exams.

- The average lump found by a first mammogram is 6 millimeters (¼ inch). Lumps this size could still be easily missed during a breast exam.
- The average lump discovered during a regular monthly BSE is 16 millimeters (⅝ inch). Many of these lumps could have been detected years sooner with a mammogram.

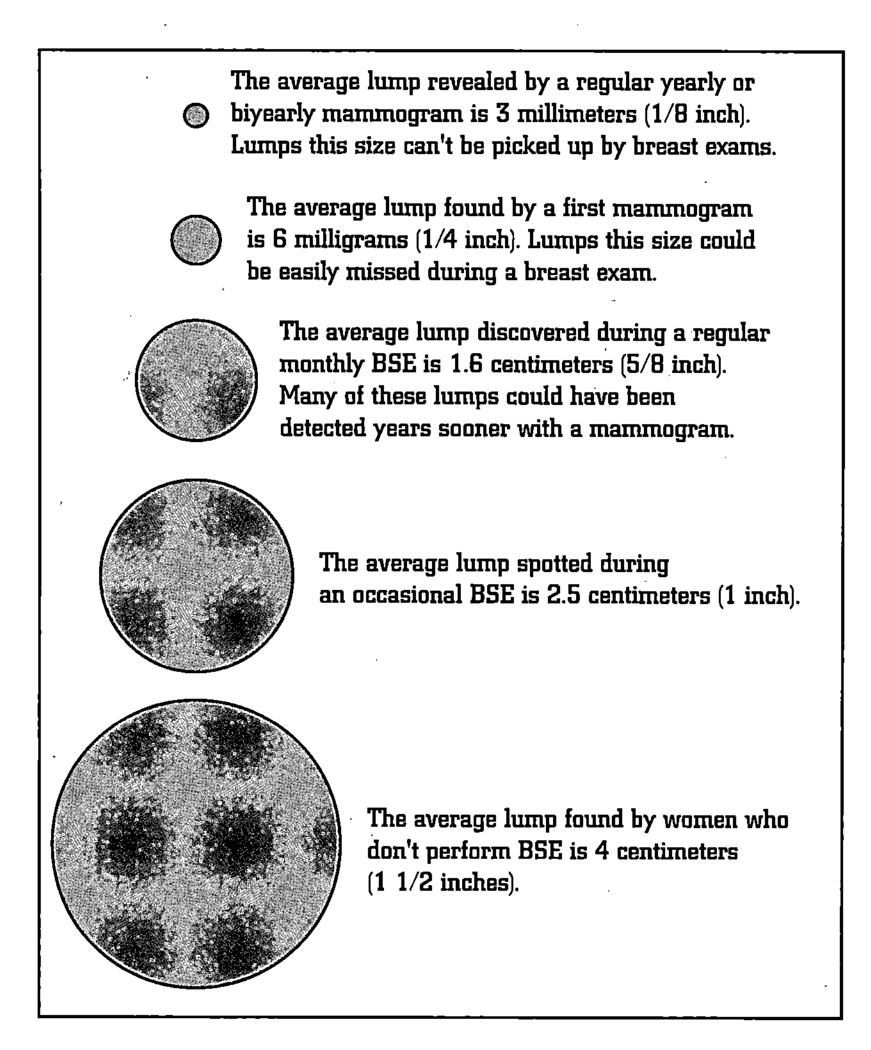

- The average lump spotted during an occasional BSE is 2.5 centimeters (1 inch).
- The average lump found in women who don't perform BSE is 4 centimeters (1½ inches).

What is cystic disease?

"Fibrocystic disease" is actually not a disease. It is a catchall term that means different things to different doctors. Some use it to describe women with noncancerous lumps such as cysts, fibroadenomas, wartlike growths, and benign tumors. Others use it to refer to women with noticeably lumpy breasts. The lumpiness typically changes with the menstrual cycle. Sometimes the breasts are tender or sore. This "condition" describes the breasts of at least half of all women in their childbearing years and is definitely not a disease. It's a perfectly normal state!

Does breast-feeding prevent cancer?

Some experts believe nursing has little or no effect on cancer prevention. Others think it may lower risk a small amount by preventing ovulation. According to the latter belief, the longer breast-feeding continues, the greater the benefit.

What is breast-cancer risk analysis?

Many women with a family history of breast cancer feel certain that they will get it, too. Some see it as an ominous shadow stalking them, and they set up their lives waiting for it to strike. Their overwhelming fear influences decisions about college, marriage, where to live, and even whether to have children.

Breast-cancer risk analysis may help them deal with their fears. It is a combination of genetic counseling, medical detective work, and a look at the statistics. When you reach adulthood, you may consider this option.

Diagnosis and Treatment

Finding a suspicious breast lump can be frightening for any woman. She may want to wish it away and pretend it doesn't exist. But she needs to find out what it is. Her next step is to consult a physician who has experience with breast cancer.

If the doctor needs a better "look" at the lump, a mammogram may be ordered. (Mammograms were discussed in Chapter Four.) Sometimes physicians will check lumps in younger women with ultrasound instead of a mammogram because the dense breast tissue of younger women renders a mammogram almost useless. Ultrasound is also used with older women to follow up on an unusual mammogram finding.

What is ultrasound?

Ultrasound is a device that transmits high-frequency sound waves through body tissues. When the sound waves encounter solid objects within the body, they bounce or echo back. You can't hear, feel, or see the sound waves, but the ultrasound device can detect them. It records the pattern of the echoes and transforms the recordings into a

photographic image on a display screen. If nothing blocks their path, the sound waves pass through the body.

Ultrasound is a painless procedure and doesn't use X rays. To allow the ultrasound transmitter/recorder to glide easily over the breast, the breast is covered with a film of jelly.

Ultrasound isn't a good screening tool—it can't consistently pick up breast lumps less than 2 centimeters (about ¾ inch) and it can be confused by normal breast lumpiness. But ultrasound can determine whether lumps detected by other means are solid or fluid-filled. The sound waves pass through fluid-filled cysts and bounce off solid ones.

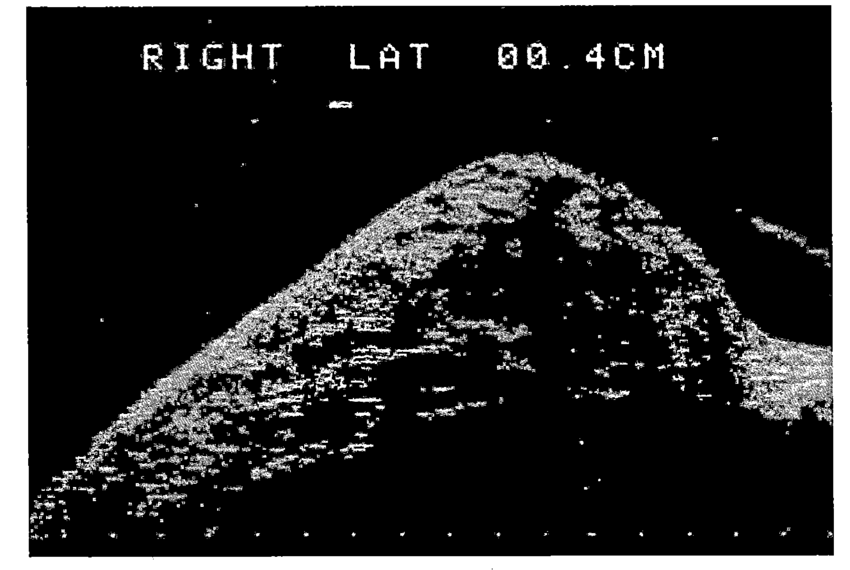

Ultrasound image of a breast lump

What is MRI?

Magnetic resonance imaging—MRI for short—is another tool that can provide a picture of the inside of the breast. It makes use of the magnetic properties of hydrogen atoms. The way it works is easy to understand. You probably know that your body is part water. You also might know that water molecules consist of two hydrogen atoms and one oxygen atom. But did you know that the nucleus of a hydrogen atom can act like a tiny magnet?

The MRI scanner is a huge magnet. It can magnetize the body's hydrogen atoms in the same way you can magnetize a paper clip with a magnet. The patient is placed in a cylinder that contains a powerful magnet. When the magnet is switched on, it creates a magnetic field. The nuclei of the hydrogen atoms line up in one direction. Then another magnetic field is turned on at right angles to the first. The nuclei begin to spin. While the nuclei spin, they send out

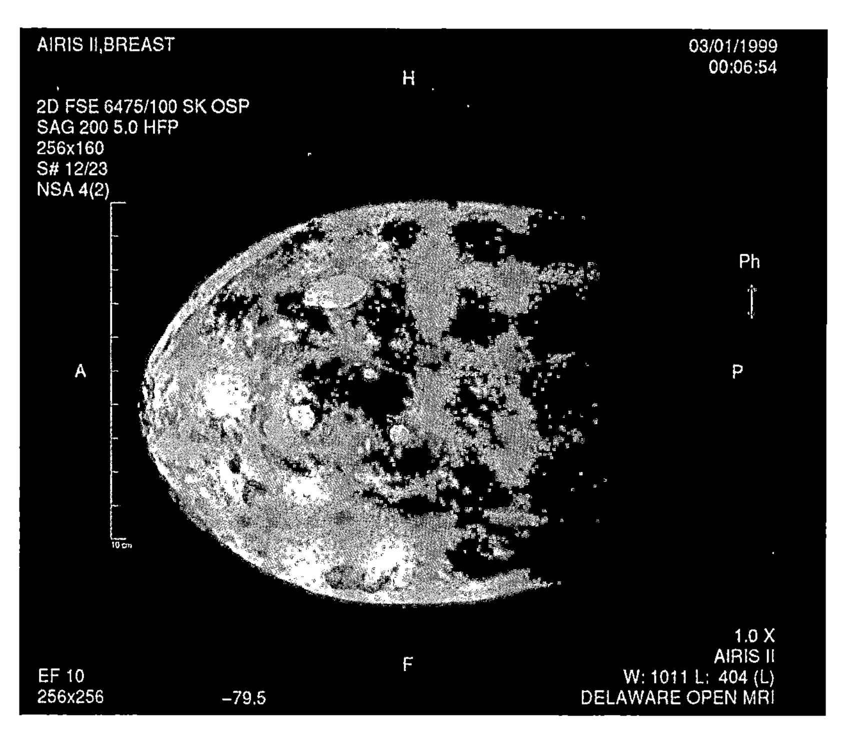

MRI of a breast

signals. A computer records and translates the signals into a picture. When the magnet is switched off, the nuclei return to normal.

Normal cells hold water more tightly than cancer cells, so the difference between the two can easily be distinguished in an MRI scan. In fact, an MRI scan can reveal a cluster of cancer cells as tiny as 3 millimeters (⅛ inch). The high cost of MRI scans, however, prohibits their everyday use as a screening tool for breast cancer.

Are doctors always right?

Doctors can usually tell by examining a lump whether it should be investigated further. However, once in a great while a physician can make a mistake. If you find a lump and your doctor dismisses your concerns, you most likely have absolutely nothing to worry about. But listen to your inner voice. You may want to consult with another doctor who has experience with breast cancer.

What is a biopsy?

If someone you know has breast cancer, her diagnosis was determined by a *biopsy* and microscopic examination of the tumor cells. In a biopsy a surgeon or radiologist removes cells or tissue from a suspicious lump in one of six ways:

Fine-needle biopsy. The surgeon or radiologist inserts a narrow needle into the lump and removes a few cells. If fluid can be extracted the lump can easily be identified as a harmless, fluid-filled cyst. This procedure can be done with ultrasound for guidance.

Core-needle biopsy. A special hollow needle is used to remove from the lump a small cylinder the size of a pencil lead. This is usually done using ultrasound or a mammogram for guidance.

Incisional biopsy. The surgeon makes a cut, or incision, in the skin and removes a large piece of the lump. This procedure is usually performed on large masses.

Excisional biopsy. The entire lump is completely removed. Surgeons perform these when lumps are small and easy to take out.

Localization biopsy. A radiologist uses a mammogram or ultrasound to precisely locate abnormalities that cannot be felt. The questionable area is marked by inserting a thin needle into the breast so the needle passes through or next to the abnormality. The surgeon then removes the needle-targeted area.

Stereotactic core biopsy. X rays of the breast are taken from two different angles to produce a three-dimensional, computer-generated picture. The computer then plots the exact location of the abnormality and guides a "biopsy gun" to the spot. Similar to an ear-piercing device, the biopsy gun shoots a needle into the suspicious area and removes some tissue. To obtain a good sample, tissue is removed from several different angles. Less tissue is taken altogether than would be excised during a surgical biopsy.

A fine-needle biopsy may be done with local anesthesia or none at all. Most biopsies, however, require local anesthesia for comfort. Local anesthesia numbs only the part of the breast with the lump. Sedatives are often given by vein to help the patient relax. In rare cases general anesthesia is used to render the patient unconscious.

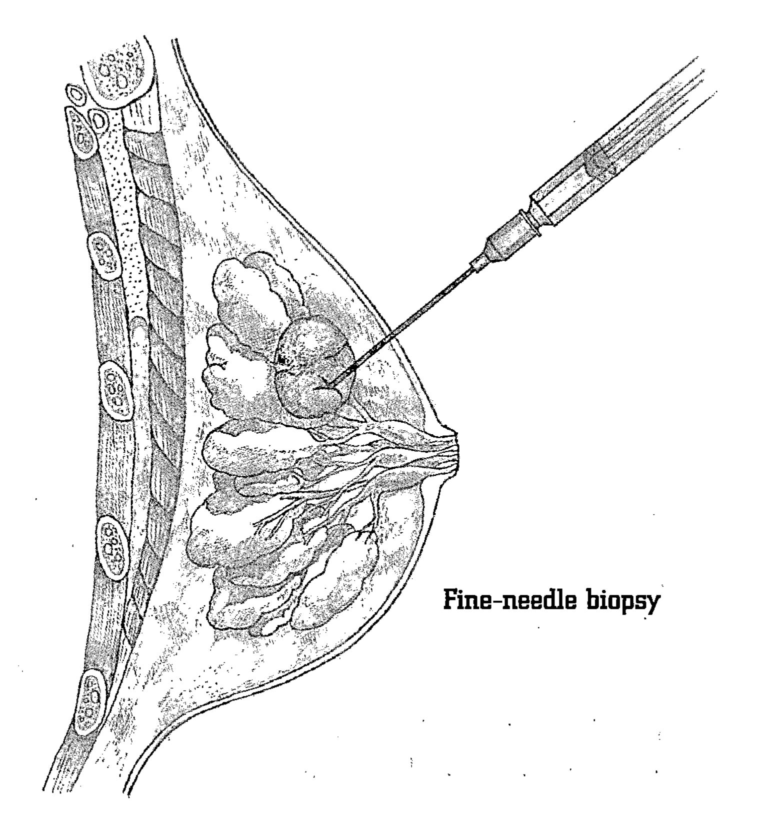

Fine-needle biopsy

After the tissue is removed, it is sent to a pathologist, a physician who studies cells to determine disease. To check for cancer, the pathologist examines the tissue under a microscope. About 80 percent of the time the findings show that a lump is harmless. This means that most women who undergo biopsies learn they are cancer-free! Many biopsies are done "just to be sure" on lumps that physicians think are probably harmless.

If a *malignancy* (cancer) is confirmed, the pathologist determines the kind of cancer present. (A discussion of the different kinds of breast cancer appears on page 44.) The pathologist will also try to establish how quickly the cells divide and if the cancer has entered blood vessels or lymph vessels. The cells will be tested to find out whether hormones affect their growth. In general, tumors that react to hormones grow more slowly than tumors that don't react.

What is staging?

Biopsies alone cannot give a complete picture of how a cancer acts in a particular woman's body. Cancer specialists devised a system called *staging* to describe how far a breast cancer has spread. Physicians use staging to make a prediction about a patient's future health and determine which treatments are best.

What tests are used to determine staging?

One of the first steps in staging a tumor is to check the lymph nodes for cancer cells. During the operation to remove the breast tumor, one or more lymph nodes beneath the arms are surgically removed and sent to the pathologist.

Underarm lymph nodes filter lymph that flows through the breast. They are one of the first places that breast cancer goes. If the lymph nodes contain cancer cells, there is a chance the cancer has spread to distant sites. (See pages 45–46 for more about lymph nodes.)

When breast-cancer cells disperse they tend to wind up in the lungs, liver, bones, or skin. They may eventually metastasize to the brain. A chest X ray can reveal if the cancer has spread to the lungs. A blood test can pick up unusual changes in the liver. A bone scan can detect areas of active tumor growth in the bones, and a *CAT scan* can uncover liver, lung, and brain tumors.

What is a bone scan?

You probably are familiar with how X rays and blood tests are performed. A *bone scan* is a little more complicated. A very small dose of a *radioactive chemical* is injected into the patient's bloodstream. The chemical gives off invisible radiation. Your eyes can't see the radiation, but special scanners can detect it.

The patient waits several hours for the chemical to be absorbed by her bone cells. Then she is scanned by a machine that counts the number of radioactive particles in her bones. It makes a picture of her skeleton that shows where the cells are most active. If the scan picks up a cluster of activity, X rays of the area can reveal whether it is caused by cancer or not. The radiation used in this chemical is very short-lived and is eliminated in the urine within five to six hours.

How does a CAT scan work?

The "CAT" in CAT scan is short for *computerized axial tomography*. This device combines X-ray and computer technology to make detailed pictures of the body's soft tissues and internal organs. It can be used to check for liver and brain tumors and is often used to obtain a more detailed image of the lungs when a chest X ray shows an abnormal finding. A CAT scan can detect tiny tumors only 2 to 3 millimeters (less than ⅛ inch) in size!

To make a CAT scan, the patient lies on a table inside a donut-shaped machine. The CAT scanner moves around

Stage	Tumor Size	Signs of Spread	Most Likely Outcome
Carcinoma in situ	Very early breast cancer.	It has not spread to nearby tissues.	It can nearly always be treated successfully by surgery alone or surgery and radiation. There is a 98%+ chance of long-term survival.
	Cancer cells are contained in the lining of the milk ducts. They can also be present in a long segment of a duct as a thin thread.	Cancer cells have not spread outside the ducts.	" "
Stage 1	Tumor is 2 cm (¾ inch) or smaller.	Lymph nodes under the arm have no cancer. The cancer has not spread beyond the breast.	Excellent chance for long-term survival.
Stage 2	Tumor is between 2 and 5 cm (about 1–2 inches).	It may—or may not—have spread to the lymph nodes under the arm. No evidence of spreading has been found in distant parts of the body.	Usually responds well to treatment. Prognosis is usually good.
	Tumor is less than 2 cm (¾ inch).	Some of the lymph nodes contain cancer.	" "

Stage	Tumor Size	Signs of Spread	Most Likely Outcome
Stage 3	Tumor is larger than 5 cm (2 inches).	No signs of cancer have been detected in distant body parts.	The cancer is more advanced but sometimes Stage 3 tumors respond well to aggressive treatment.
	Tumor can be any size and has invaded the chest the chest wall.	" "	" "
	The tumor can be any size, and the cancer has spread to lymph nodes under the arm. The nodes have become stuck to the chest wall under the arm.	" "	" "
	The tumor can be any size and has spread to lymph nodes above the collarbone.	" "	" "
Stage 4	Tumor can be any size.	Cancer has spread to other parts of the body.	These cancers are usually not curable, but often they can be slowed with treatment.

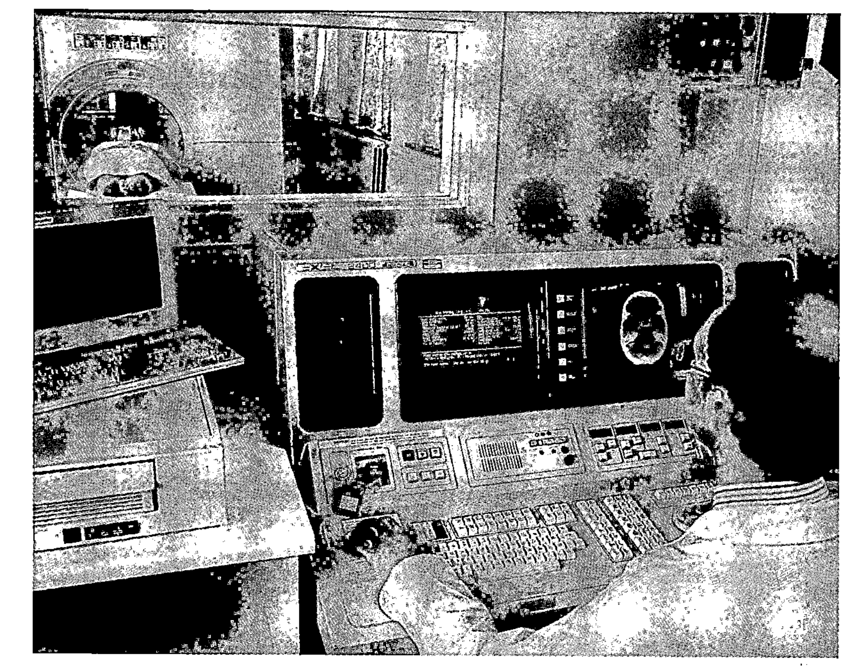

A CAT scanner

the patient, sending narrow X-ray beams through the body at different angles. A detector in the machine picks up the information revealed by the X rays. A computer then translates the information into a series of cross sections. The resulting pictures look like "slices" of the patient's body. CAT scans provide a better image than plain X rays, but they also expose the body to more radiation. They are used only when all other tests are inconclusive.

Can the information taken from the biopsy, blood tests, X rays, bone scan, MRI, and CAT scan prove that the cancer has not spread?

All these tests can confirm the spread of cancer by revealing a mass of cancer. But they cannot prove that the cancer has not spread. They lack the ability to find individual stray cancer cells. So far, no method exists to establish conclusively that cancer cells have not metastasized. That's why regular checkups are important for breast-cancer patients.

What are the treatment options for breast cancer?

After cancer has been confirmed, the doctor and patient agree upon a plan of treatment. This plan is called a *protocol.* It depends mainly on the stage of the cancer. At the time this book was written, four main kinds of treatments existed: surgery, radiation therapy, chemotherapy, and hormone therapy. These options will be explained shortly. Perhaps by the time you read this, new and better treatments will be available.

Where can a woman find a second opinion?

Before beginning breast-cancer treatment, many women seek out a second cancer specialist to review their diagnosis and treatment plan. There are several different ways to get a second opinion:

- A woman's doctor may recommend another specialist.
- A woman can ask her doctor to discuss her case with another physician.
- She may consult directly with another physician herself.
- To find the name of another specialist, a woman can ask friends for referrals or check with her hospital or local medical society.

What are the surgical options for breast cancer today?

If someone you know was diagnosed with breast cancer, she probably had surgery to remove as much of the cancer as possible. These are the common options for breast-cancer surgery today:

- **Lumpectomy.** This procedure enables a woman to keep her breast. The surgeon removes the cancerous lump along with the rim of normal tissues surrounding it. The extra tissue is taken to ensure the complete removal of all cancer cells. One or more lymph nodes may be taken through a separate incision so they can be checked.
- **Modified radical mastectomy.** The surgeon removes the entire breast and some or all of the underarm lymph nodes. This operation does not leave a hollow in the chest.
- **Simple mastectomy.** This is similar to the modified radical mastectomy, but usually no lymph nodes are removed.

Sometimes chemotherapy is given prior to a lumpectomy to make the tumor smaller. If the tumor shrinks, less

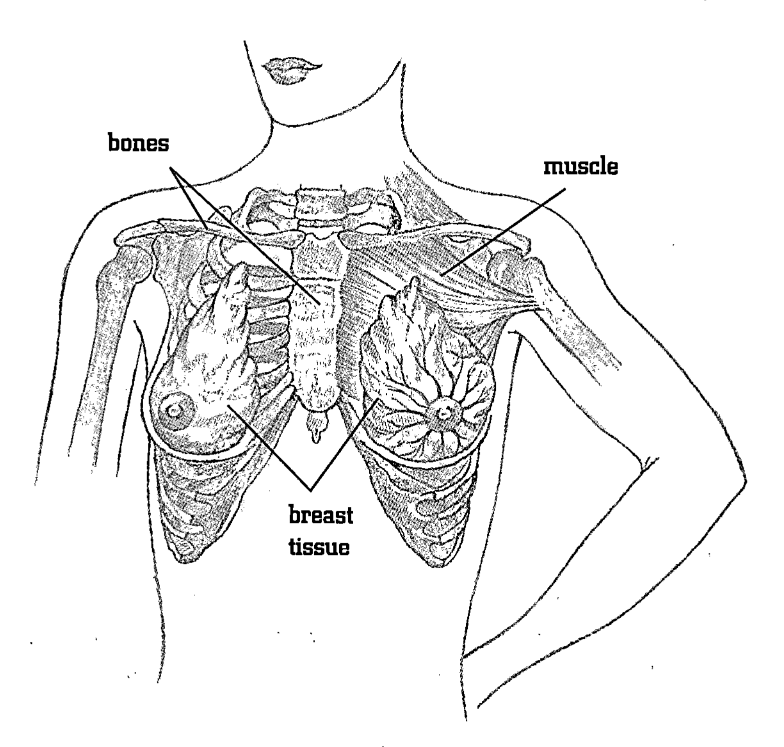

breast tissue needs to be removed. To make sure no cancer cells remain in the breast after a lumpectomy, women usually undergo radiation treatment. Studies show that lumpectomies followed by radiation treatment are just as effective as mastectomies when the tumors are small.

What was the treatment in the past?

Beginning in 1894 and lasting for more than seventy years, the standard treatment for breast cancer was a *radical mastectomy*. In this operation the surgeon removed the entire breast, the chest muscles beneath the breast, and all the underarm lymph nodes. It left a woman with a hollow in her chest and a blow to her self-image.

The rationale for the radical mastectomy was the belief that breast cancer advanced in a predictable order. Supposedly, it began in the breast, spread to the lymph nodes under the arm, and then traveled to other parts of the body. The radical mastectomy was intended to stop its progress.

However, research revealed that breast-cancer cells can start to roam early. They may break off from the tumor and be whisked by the blood or lymph to distant organs. This made it clear that bigger and more radical breast surgery no longer made sense. In the 1970s less drastic surgery began to replace the radical mastectomy. The emphasis in treatment shifted to saving as much of the breast and surrounding tissue as possible while controlling the spread of cancer with chemotherapy and radiation.

Does the loss of underarm lymph nodes and lymph vessels cause lasting problems?

The loss of underarm lymph nodes and their connecting vessels may slow lymph circulation in the affected arm. As a result, the arm may swell. However, with today's surgical and radiation techniques, this is uncommon. Women with mastectomies must protect the affected arm from injury for the rest of their lives to reduce the risk of swelling. Swollen tissue is more prone to infection. Women with lumpectomies who had lymph nodes removed must also be careful.

Is it necessary to remove so many lymph nodes?

In the late 1990s a new procedure was developed to determine whether breast cancer had spread to the lymph nodes. It involves injecting the tissue around the tumor site with a dye or radioactive tracer. The dye or tracer leaves the site, following the path that cancerous cells might take to the lymph nodes. The surgeon tracks the movement and removes the first lymph node that the dye or tracer reaches. The node is checked for cancer. If it is cancer-free, then it is presumed that the remaining nodes are cancer-free, too. They are left alone. However, if the first node proves to be cancerous, the other nodes are removed. Occasionally, extra radiation to the underarm is added to the treatment regime, and the nodes are spared.

Is surgery used to treat widespread cancer?

Sometimes tumors press against nerves, organs, or bones, creating pain or even blocking a vital function. Removing the tumor will make the patient feel better but unfortunately will not cure the cancer. Chemotherapy and/or radiation are used when the cancer is widespread.

What is radiation therapy?

Radiation therapy begins three to seven weeks after surgery or follows chemotherapy if chemo is used. Radiation therapy utilizes high-powered, invisible rays from an X-ray machine to damage cancer cells and prevent them from reproducing. Radiation therapy is an effective weapon, but it acts only in the area receiving the radiation. It isn't used to treat the whole body because it can hurt healthy cells, too.

Radiation therapy

Radiation therapy works best against scattered small tumor cells left in the breast after a lumpectomy. It may also be used to treat advanced breast cancer in other parts of the body. By shrinking large tumors, radiation therapy eases pain.

Radiation therapy creates some unpleasant side effects. The skin over the treated area may become "sunburned," and a rash may appear. The patient may feel tired—as though she has spent the day sunbathing at the beach. These side effects disappear when the treatments are finished. Most women have little trouble with radiation therapy and can work full-time and participate in most of their usual activities on the days they receive treatment. The most difficult aspect of radiation therapy may be the time involved. The patient must go for treatment five days a week for six weeks.

What is chemotherapy?

Chemotherapy is a treatment that uses powerful drugs to fight cancer cells. These drugs can be taken by pill, injection, or intravenously (by IV). The drugs circulate in the bloodstream to places where cancer cells may be hiding in the body.

Anti-cancer drugs act in one or more of the following ways. They:

- sabotage cell growth
- block cell division
- interfere with the cell's nutrition uptake and "starve" the cell to death

As a cancer evolves, some of its cells may mutate again and again. As a result, tumors often contain different kinds of cancer cells. A drug that works against one type may be ineffective against the others. A combination of anticancer drugs provides the best treatment. Where one drug fails, another drug may succeed.

Unfortunately, anti-cancer drugs aren't choosy. They destroy some healthy, rapidly growing cells, too. That's why they may cause side effects such as hair loss, nausea and vomiting, fever, loss of appetite, diarrhea, mouth sores, inflamed eyes, tiredness, and a flulike feeling. The side effects depend on the type of drug, and vary from patient to patient. Not every patient becomes violently ill. But for those who do, special medication may ease their discomfort. Many effective anti-nausea drugs exist.

Chemotherapy frequently affects *bone marrow,* the innermost part of bone where blood cells develop. During treatment, fewer red blood cells, platelets, and white blood cells will form. As a result a patient may be pale and exhausted. She may bruise or bleed more easily. She will also be more prone to serious infection. However, new drugs that promote the rapid replenishment of blood cells can help the patient's immune system recover more quickly.

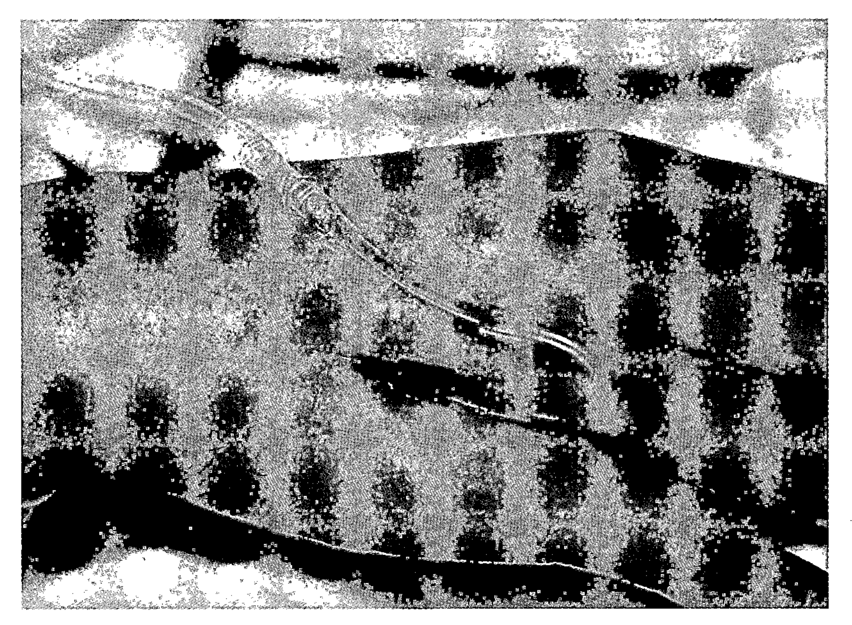

Medicine given by IV drips from a container into a tube. The tube connects to a needle that empties into a vein.

Patients who undergo chemotherapy may be embarrassed about their appearance, especially if they lose their hair temporarily. They may want to avoid visitors even though they need the encouragement of family and friends. If you know someone who is receiving chemotherapy and feels this way, try to accept her appearance. Look her in the eye and try to see the person you care about, not the changes. This may help her feel more comfortable. If she hasn't done so already, you might encourage her to wear a stylish wig, turban, or scarf.

Typically, chemotherapy is given over a period of three to six months, although four months may be enough. During this time the patient's *oncologist*—a doctor who specializes in cancer treatment—will watch her carefully. The oncologist wants to make sure the cancer drugs don't inflict any permanent damage. Many women can keep up with many of their usual activities during the course of chemotherapy treatments. Side effects usually disappear when treatment ends. The nausea stops, hair grows back, and bone marrow returns to normal. The patient feels better and acts more like her old self.

With such nasty side effects, why is chemotherapy given?

To put it simply, the payoff makes it worthwhile. Chemotherapy prolongs life and often decreases the chance of the cancer returning. Chemotherapy probably fails to kill every stray tumor cell, but it may reduce the cancer to a level that the patient's immune system can handle. The role of the immune system will be discussed in Chapter Eight.

Why doesn't chemotherapy cure all cancer?

Some cancer cells may be *resistant* to the chemotherapy. The anti-cancer drugs will not destroy them. The cancer cells may be resistant to a drug from the outset, or the cancer may develop resistance over time. Some women have a better response to hormone therapy.

How does hormone therapy work?

Almost two-thirds of all breast cancers require the hormone estrogen to grow. On the surface of these cancer cells lie structures called *receptors*, which control the entry of estrogen. Various treatments exist to cut off the cells' access to estrogen. The most common is the drug *tamoxifen.*

Tamoxifen becomes part of the surface of breast-cancer cells. It jams the receptors and keeps the cells from acquiring the estrogen they need. Somehow tamoxifen also disrupts the cells' life cycle, causing them to die. Tamoxifen produces some side effects, but they are much less severe than those caused by chemotherapy. Tamoxifen users, especially those over the age of fifty, have an increased risk of developing blood clots in the veins, and an increased risk for endometrial cancer. (The endometrium is the lining of the uterus.) New drugs, similar to tamoxifen, are described in Chapter Eight.

Preventive surgery—the removal of the ovaries—eliminates the major source of female hormones in the body and starves tumor cells of estrogen. In the past it was the only option for younger women with advanced cancer. Now younger women can be treated with tamoxifen or chemotherapy. Chemotherapy causes many women to enter menopause early. But tamoxifen does not stop estrogen production. Younger women using tamoxifen may become pregnant if they are sexually active and don't use birth control.

What is breast reconstruction?

To replace a missing breast, many women undergo surgery to construct a new one. Often, this surgery is performed during the same operation as a mastectomy. Some patients wait six months or more after a mastectomy to complete radiation or chemotherapy treatments before reconstruction. Not all women choose reconstructive surgery, which carries its own set of risks.

Several options exist for breast reconstruction:

- **Implant placement.** A sack filled with a saline solution—salt and water—is placed under the chest muscle. In the past, implants filled with silicone gel were commonly used. The government restricted their use after there was concern about health problems attributed to leaking implants. Saline implants may leak, too, but their contents are harmless and will be absorbed by the body. Of course, a leaky implant will need to be replaced as it will flatten like a deflated balloon. Researchers are looking into other kinds of materials to use in implants that are as safe as saline but have a more natural texture.
- **Tissue transfer from the back.** A back muscle is used as a replacement for the breast tissue removed. An

implant is placed beneath the muscle. Fat and skin from the back cover the muscle.

- **Tissue transfer from the abdomen.** One muscle from the abdomen is transplanted to the chest along with fat and skin. They are positioned to take on the shape of a breast.
- **Microsurgery.** In a delicate surgery, tissue covering the abdomen or buttocks is moved and its blood vessels are reconnected to create a new breast.

A new areola and nipple can usually be created from skin on the upper thigh. Although a reconstructed breast looks like a breast, it lacks the sensations of one. If it is stroked the woman doesn't feel the touch in the way she once did. The new breast also lacks milk glands, so it cannot nurse a baby. But it helps a woman look more like her old self in and out of clothes. It also has the softness of her original breast.

Is reconstruction necessary?

No! Some women with mastectomies choose not to have reconstructive surgery. Many of them opt to wear an artificial breast—a *prosthesis*. Like breasts, prostheses come in many shapes and sizes. Women can buy special bras to hold the prosthesis, or they can sew a pocket in a regular bra or bathing suit to accommodate it. One kind of prosthesis mimics the weight and feel of a breast. It uses an adhesive to stick to the chest and doesn't slip. But the adhesive can cause skin irritation, so it's not right for everyone.

Some small-breasted women never bother with a prosthesis. When dressed, there is little difference in their appearance, and they are satisfied with the way they look. Others shun prostheses because they find them to be uncomfortable.

Some women feel no need to hide the fact of their surgery. They successfully ignore the pressure to conform to society's expectations of what is "womanly." For these women, having the appearance of two breasts is not vital to their self-esteem, and they have no desire to hide their breast-cancer experience. However, there are drawbacks to this option. It's like wearing a sign that announces they have a history of breast cancer. When these women meet new people, their medical status comes immediately into focus, and other qualities they possess may become secondary.

A few women have used their mastectomy scars to make a political statement about breast cancer. Matuschka, an artist who lost her right breast to cancer, uses nude self-portraits to shock viewers. Her art forces people to confront the devastating impact of breast cancer. She and other activists want the U.S. government to pour more money into much-needed breast-cancer research.

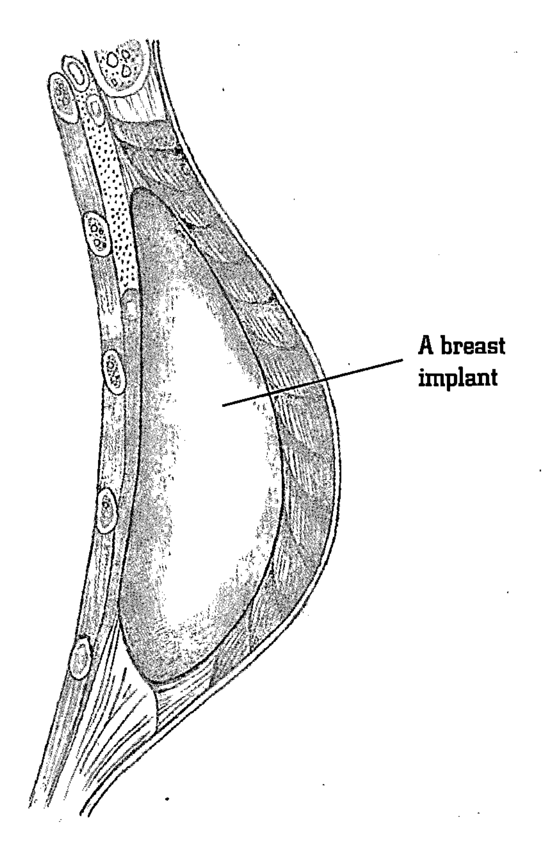

The choice to undergo reconstructive surgery, wear a prosthesis, or do nothing is highly personal and up to each individual woman. There is no right or wrong.

Can a woman who has had breast cancer still have sex?

Nothing prevents a woman who has had breast cancer from having a fulfilling sex life. A loving relationship is built on trust, common interests, and shared experiences as well as mutual attraction. Having sex will not make the cancer come back or spread faster. Her partner cannot catch cancer by touching, kissing, or sucking a breast.

After losing a breast some women have difficulty with intimacy because they don't feel good about themselves. They need time to regain their self-worth and learn they can still be beautiful without a breast. A supportive partner can be vital in a woman's adjustment to her new status.

Can a woman who has had breast cancer still have children?

Deciding to have children is a difficult choice for young women who have had breast cancer. They worry that they will not live long enough to raise their children. They wonder whether pregnancy hormones will make their cancer reappear.

No one can predict how pregnancy will affect any individual patient. Women who become pregnant after breast-cancer treatment seem to have the same chance of long-term survival as women who don't. This means that some of these new mothers will live to see their children grow up, but sadly, others will not.

So how does a woman choose? She needs to consider her diagnosis and prognosis. Pregnancy hormones cannot cause cancer to spread, but they may fuel the growth of stray cancer cells that are hormone-sensitive. A woman whose lymph nodes contained cancer must decide if giving birth is worth the risk. But a woman whose cancer was found very early has an excellent chance of seeing her children grow and have children of their own.

Can a woman who had breast cancer nurse a baby?

The healthy breast will still produce milk in a woman with a history of breast cancer. If the woman underwent radiation treatment following a lumpectomy, she will be unable to nurse in the affected breast. Radiation treatment damages milk-producing tissue.

Can a pregnant woman develop breast cancer?

A very small percentage of breast cancers occur in pregnant women. These cancers are difficult to detect because breasts thicken and become lumpier during pregnancy. Most lumps that arise in pregnancy are harmless. In rare cases they can mask a cancerous change and delay diagnosis and treatment. Women should examine their breasts monthly while pregnant and discuss any unusual findings with their health-care providers.

If a suspicious lump turns up, an ultrasound and biopsy can be performed with little risk to the unborn child. If breast cancer is found, treatment will depend on the stage of the pregnancy. General anesthesia poses a slight risk of injury to the fetus, but surgery is an option at any time. The use of radiation treatment, however, is hazardous to the fetus and cannot be administered at all during the pregnancy. Chemotherapy cannot be given during the first trimester (first three months) of pregnancy but can be given safely after that.

Some women who learn in the first trimester that they have breast cancer opt to have a mastectomy and continue with their pregnancies. Women who learn about their cancer during the second and third trimesters of pregnancy can sometimes have a lumpectomy or mastectomy followed by chemotherapy. After the baby is born radiation treatment can be given.

The cancer itself poses no threat to the baby. Breast-cancer cells cannot spread to it. To treat the mother sooner, the baby may be delivered early by *cesarean section* when it is able to live on its own.

Some women with aggressive breast cancers may be advised to terminate their pregnancies, so the cancer can be treated aggressively. Some women may feel safer if the pregnancy is terminated. Deciding whether to end a pregnancy or not is a difficult choice.

Does breast cancer occur in nursing mothers?

Nursing mothers can develop breast cancer, but it doesn't happen very often. The changes due to breast-feeding make the disease hard to detect. If a nursing mother finds an unusual and persistent lump, her physician should check it out. If a biopsy reveals breast cancer, the baby can be switched to bottle feeding, and treatment can begin immediately. Incidentally, the mother cannot pass cancer to the baby through her milk.

What is remission?

Breast cancer that spreads to distant parts of the body can rarely be cured, but it can seem to disappear. This *remission* can last for months or years before the cancer flares up again. The longer a cancer stays in remission before reappearing, the more treatable it will be. Many women who have had breast cancer live to an old age and die of other causes.

What happens if breast cancer reappears?

If breast cancer comes back, the treatment will depend on:

- the location of the cancer
- whether it's widespread

- if the patient still menstruates or not
- the patient's overall health
- how the patient reacted to the initial therapy

If the disease returns to the same breast after a lumpectomy and radiation treatment, a mastectomy and possibly a *systemic* treatment, such as chemotherapy or hormone therapy, will be recommended. Surgery, radiation, and systemic therapy may all be recommended if the recurrence occurs on the chest wall after a mastectomy.

Breast cancer rarely spreads from one breast to the other. If it develops in the unaffected breast, it will be treated like a new cancer. If the cancer turns up in other parts of the body, chemotherapy and hormone therapy may be prescribed. In this case, surgery and radiation therapy may also be implemented to slow its progress and relieve pain.

What is a bone marrow transplant?

Bone marrow transplantation therapy is being tested for its effectiveness against advanced cancers. It involves treating the patient with ultrahigh doses of chemotherapy, so powerful that they destroy the patient's bone marrow and, it is hoped, the cancer. The patient is then given bone marrow to rebuild her immune system. However, so far there is no proof that this procedure is any better than standard chemotherapy in saving lives.

Can breast cancer be cured?

Fortunately, breast cancer can be cured when it is caught early. But women with advanced cancer should not abandon hope. Medical researchers continually seek more effective treatments for early and advanced cancers. The lives of breast-cancer patients are being extended with new approaches to treatment. Chapter Eight describes current research that may lead to a cure in the future.

Chapter Six

Coping When a Mother Has Breast Cancer

If your mother had breast cancer, do you remember how you felt when you first learned about it? If you were old enough to understand the serious nature of the disease, you probably felt numb or shocked. You couldn't believe what was happening. Perhaps a zillion thoughts seemed to swirl in your brain, and you couldn't focus on a single one. Or maybe your mind just seemed to shut down completely.

After the news sank in, you may have wondered: "Why me? Why my mother? Who will take care of me?" Suddenly, your life had changed. Something terrible was happening, and you had no control over it. Even worse, you mother could not control events either. You felt like your life would never be normal again.

When cancer strikes it affects the whole family. Everybody worries whether the patient will get better or not, but each individual may react differently. Family members may feel tense, angry, helpless, afraid, sad, confused, or lonely. Some may withdraw; others may talk nonstop. Some may become quarrelsome; others may act as though nothing is wrong. You may even wonder if anybody else but you cares that your mother is sick.

If you don't understand why the people around you act the way they do, ask them—nicely. You cannot change the fact that your family is upset. But by talking things out you may be able to understand everybody's feelings —and yourself—better.

Why am I so angry?

Adults are supposed to be in control! Moms, especially, aren't supposed to get sick—at least that's what most kids would like to believe. When your mother became ill, it may have felt like a betrayal. After all, it's the mom's responsibility to take care of the kids, right? Many households depend on the mom to do almost everything. She shops and prepares meals, takes care of laundry and cleaning, runs car pools, helps with homework, and reminds kids to eat right, brush their teeth, and pick up after themselves. It's normal to feel angry when you feel you have been let down.

Sometimes anger masks feelings of fear or helplessness. It may be easier to act angry and pick fights than to admit you feel scared or helpless.

You may also be upset because your family expects you to pick up your mother's slack. Suddenly, your mother's chores become your problem. You may be expected to help her out—bring her meals, get her water, fetch a book, answer the phone, watch younger siblings—little tasks that may add up to one big bother. Just when you are reaching the age when you want to spend more time with friends and become more independent, you are suddenly being sucked right back into the family. No wonder you're upset!

To make matters worse, you may begin to resent your mom and become impatient with her. You probably show it. You might even explode and yell at her. And then what happens? You feel guilty.

You are not alone. Many kids whose mothers have breast cancer or any other serious illness become angry at their mothers for getting sick and disrupting their lives. Some kids become upset because they think they are expected to do too much. Others are furious because they may have to live somewhere else while their mothers are in the hospital. Still others react to parents who themselves are acting angry, impatient, or unfair. Getting angry is a natural reaction. It doesn't mean that you don't love your mom or that you are a terrible daughter.

How do I deal with my anger?

The first step in controlling anger is to become aware that it is building before you explode. If you feel yourself getting upset, ask yourself why. Are you hungry? Tired? Lonely? Frustrated? Scared? Feeling unappreciated? Reacting to someone else's anger? Could this be PMS? (Refer to page 31 for more information on PMS.)

To avoid a blowup, call for a time-out to cool down. Seek the solitude of your room, or take a walk to collect your thoughts. Some people find exercise to be a constructive outlet. If you leave the house, tell somebody where you are headed. You don't want to heap worry onto an already tense situation.

You can use *visualization* to soothe your anger. Picture a peaceful scene in your mind, perhaps a beach or mountaintop. Put yourself in the picture and walk around. What do you see, hear, touch, and smell? Continue to explore until you feel calm again. Prayer or meditation may also help you find peace.

If you use anger to protect yourself from feeling sad, fearful, helpless, guilty, or other troubling emotions, you need to let out these feelings. The best way is to find someone with whom you can talk. This is especially true if you are frightened that your mother's fate will be your own. Speak with your father or choose a friend who will listen and respect your confidence by not sharing your worries with others.

How can I regain control of my life?

Learn how to solve problems constructively. If something is bothering you, identify the problem and write it down. Then list several of your options. Next to each one, note its good and bad points. After weighing your options, draw up a plan of action. Set a deadline to put the plan in place and then DO IT!

How can I reduce stress?

Keeping healthy and fit is a key to reducing stress. If you eat properly and get enough sleep you will be better equipped to handle difficult situations. Exercise at least twenty minutes a day, three to seven times a week, to work out tension, anger, and depression. You needn't do anything elaborate—a brisk walk or a bike ride will suffice.

Whom can I talk to?

It's hard to constantly put up a brave front all by yourself. You need to find one or more people to help you through this difficult time. Finding someone to listen to you and support you may feel scary in itself, especially if in the past you confided your big worries to your mom.

Try your father first, but if this is not possible make a list of people you respect. This list may include grandparents, aunts, uncles, cousins, teachers, neighbors, friends of your parents, parents of your friends, a rabbi, minister, or priest, guidance counselor, school nurse, scout leader, coach, older sibling, friends, or a former baby-sitter.

Choose one or more people who seem to be good listeners and who you think will answer questions honestly. Then telephone, e-mail, or visit them. If you're not sure what to say, you can always start out with news about your mom. You can then gauge from the response whether you will feel comfortable confiding in the person or not. You will find that some people know just what to say and are sensitive to your feelings. Others have no understanding of what you are going through, and this may make you may feel worse. Keep looking until you find someone with whom you feel comfortable.

A support group with other children of cancer patients can provide an excellent source of strength and comfort. These groups provide a safe setting for kids to talk about their worries and share their experiences. Many hospitals provide support groups for families of cancer patients. If your mother's hospital does not, the American Cancer Society can tell you where to find a support group. Their toll-free number is 1-800-227-2345.

Sometimes belonging to a support group or sharing feelings with someone you trust is not enough. If you have extra problems or concerns that you can't work out, a social worker, psychologist, nurse therapist, or family therapist may be your best bet for help. The nurses or doctors at your mother's hospital should be able to refer you to a good one.

Why are some of my friends dropping me?

When your mom was first diagnosed with cancer most of your friends probably felt sorry for you, but now some of them may be leaving you alone. This happens to lots of kids in your situation.

Some friends may not know what to say or do around you. Others may feel embarrassed or uneasy when they visit your home and see your mother looking ill. Her appearance may scare them, or they may mistakenly think they can pick up cancer germs!

You could be acting a little weird, too, because of the stress you are feeling. Your friends may think you don't want to spend time with them anymore. Hard as it may seem, the only thing you can do is reach out to your friends and explain how you feel. You may need to tell them how to be your friend right now.

If you lose friends, you will be able to make new ones. Perhaps you know someone in school who has already had experience with a very sick parent. That person probably understands what you are going through now.

Your mother may also be having difficulties with her friends. She may be disappointed if they don't make the effort to "be there" for her while she is ill. Some of her friends may want to help but do not know how to offer. Others might be "fair-weather friends"—people who can share good times but lack the maturity to help out in the bad. They may be reluctant to visit a sick person because they are afraid to think about illness and death.

Nobody tells me anything—how do I find out what's going on?

Some parents are too wrapped up in their own concerns to tell their kids what is happening. Others try to protect their children by withholding information. They may think the truth might be too painful or that the child is not old enough to handle it. Not knowing, however, can be worse than anything. If you feel left out, make a list of questions that you need to have answered. Go over the list with your parents if you can. If this is not possible, ask another adult whom you trust. If your mother's doctor or nurses seem friendly you might approach them for answers.

Try to learn all you can about breast cancer. One good way is to read books about it, but make sure the information is current. Check the copyright date on the inside of the book. If it is more than a few years old, some of the cancer information may be out-of-date.

For more current information, try these women's magazines: *Glamour, Ladies' Home Journal, Redbook, McCall's, Vogue,* and *Good Housekeeping.* They do a good job of reporting on breast cancer. Their up-to-date articles are written in a clear, easy-to-understand style. To identify recent back issues that will be useful, look under "breast cancer" in your library's *Reader's Guide to Periodical Literature,* or your library's computerized or microfilmed magazine indexes. If you need help using any of these indexes, or finding the articles, ask your librarian. While you are in the library, find out if it stocks any videos about breast cancer, too.

If you still have questions, you can call the National Cancer Institute Information Service. Their information specialists can answer questions and send you additional information. The toll-free number is: 1-800-422-6237. Volunteers at the American Cancer Society can provide information, too. Again, their toll-free number is 1-800-227-2345.

What is happening to my mother emotionally?

Your mother is being hit with a double whammy. Having cancer forces her to confront her own mortality, no matter how good her prognosis. Death stops being something that happens only to other people; she realizes that someday she will die. Even though more women survive breast cancer than ever before, virtually all women who receive a diagnosis of breast cancer feel for some period of time like they are staring death in the face.

Breast cancer also assaults your mother's sense of self, especially if a mastectomy was necessary. She is saying good-bye to the woman she thought she was and is confronting a new reality. For a while, she may not feel like she is a whole woman. She may wonder if she'll ever feel attractive again. As she copes with her sense of loss, she may feel that her body has betrayed her. She may feel all alone and believe that nobody in the whole world understands how she feels.

Your mother must also adjust to an invasion of her privacy. To battle cancer, she has to allow many different people to look at and touch her breasts. She may begin to feel as though she is less of a person as her medical team focuses on her breasts and fails to see her as a whole human being. Some members of the team may even begin to treat her like a child because she's so dependent on them and this may diminish her self-esteem further.

Everything in your mother's life has changed. She has changed. She may be coping with fatigue, pain, arm swelling, hair loss, as well as the removal of a breast. This loss of control over her body and the disruption of her routine may make her feel helpless and frustrated. On top of this the cancer treatment may make her feel plain lousy or violently ill.

Your mother may be just as frightened and angry as you are. She may think she is letting her family down and worry about how you are coping. She is probably concerned that she passed a tendency for breast cancer on to you.

With all your mother has to work through, it should be no surprise if she acts cranky, sad, depressed, withdrawn, angry, tired, or totally involved with herself. Yet knowing why she behaves strangely doesn't make it easier for you if motherhood has sunk to the bottom of her priority list. This may be especially difficult if at times your mother doesn't want to talk to you or acts as though she doesn't care. Remember, despite all the changes, deep down your mother still loves you very much.

What is happening to my family?

Your mother's illness impacts on all the members of your family. Everybody is hurting, but they all express their pain in their own individual way. You may find it scary to see your parents cry or your siblings act out by becoming defiant, bossy, or belligerent.

Your father may be so focused on your mother's needs that he lacks the energy to meet yours, especially if he's shuttling back and forth to the hospital or clinic. You may rarely eat meals together as a family, and nobody may be home to help with your homework, drive you to see your friends, or provide a listening ear. As result you may feel left out or neglected. Remember, your mother is the focus of attention because she needs it, not because you are less loved.

It would be wonderful if catastrophe brought out the best in every family member. But often the opposite occurs—people become more short-tempered and impatient with one another. Their worst traits may become exaggerated, or they may retreat into themselves. To keep things in perspective, remember that your family had its ups and downs before your mother got cancer.

You are having a hard enough time sorting out your own feelings without having to figure out what is going on in everybody else's head. Yet you will have an easier time if you understand their thinking. Family meetings can soothe tempers by giving each person a chance to express his or her concerns. This is especially important if you or one of your siblings has become overly bossy, or if you feel you are being nagged constantly one day and totally ignored the next. Keep in mind that not every argument is worth winning. It won't hurt you to give in every once in a while.

Sitting down together and reassigning responsibilities may help the household run with less friction. If money is a problem, brainstorm ways to spend less. Devise a "time-out" signal so people can cool down when tempers flare.

I feel like I am responsible for my mother's cancer. How can I stop feeling guilty?

In anger, did you ever tell your mom that you wished she was dead? Did she ever say, "You'll be the death of me," or "You make me sick"? Conflicts between mothers and daughters are as natural as thunderstorms and rain. Your mom probably experienced the same kind of fights with her mother! Words may be powerful weapons in arguments, but they don't cause cancer. Nothing you said, did, or thought made your mother sick. You don't have the power to give someone cancer.

If your mother or father pays less attention to you or snaps at you more often, you may mistakenly believe that you've done something terribly wrong. Their change in behavior reflects their worry and preoccupation with the cancer and how it has impacted on their lives. It is not your punishment for making your mother sick.

If I am super good will my mother get better?

You also don't have the power to heal your mother. Whether or not you are the perfect child will make no difference in your mother's fight against cancer. Being super good all the time will only add to your own stress. Just be yourself.

I can feel normal one moment and be crying the next. How can I control my mood swings?

Mood swings plague most teenagers because adolescents react intensely to inner and outer influences. Often they magnify problems way out of proportion to reality. It's common to be on top of the world one moment and down in the pits the next.

To control your mood swings better, put your feelings into words instead of acting out. Keep a journal or record your feelings on audio or videotape. Try to describe what you are feeling to a parent or a friend.

Some things are worth crying about. Being scared for your mother and worrying about yourself are reason enough. Perhaps you can find a safe time or place to release your tears without embarrassment.

Is it normal to feel sorry for myself?

It's okay to feel sorry for yourself. Since your mom got cancer nothing in your life seems to be the same, and your parents can't give you the attention you need. But remember you are not helpless. If you feel lonely, find someone with whom you can share your thoughts. If you believe too much responsibility has been shifted onto you, discuss this with your parents. If you imagine you are the only girl who has a mother with cancer, go to the library and finds books about other kids who have dealt with similar situations. You can also go online and check out the breast-cancer Web sites designed especially for kids. Some of these Web sites are listed in the Resources section on pages 166–169.

Remember, when you read about other cancer patients and their families, don't assume that what happens to them will happen to your family. Each cancer patient and each family is unique.

Is it normal to cling to my mother? I am afraid something bad will happen if I am not there.

You cannot protect your mother from her cancer or from the side effects of treatment. Remember, more women are living with breast cancer and living longer than in the past. Researchers are working on new ways to treat cancer and prolong life.

Why do I laugh when my mother tries to talk to me about her cancer?

Some people handle emotionally charged situations by laughing. Laughter may be your outlet for nervousness. Or, it may be your way of showing you are not yet ready to talk about cancer. Perhaps you are afraid of what your mother might tell you. Confront your fear by listing on paper the worst things she could say. Go over the list with your father or somebody else you trust. You might find that you have been scaring yourself needlessly. Then find out what your mom needs to share.

What can I do to make hospital visits more pleasant?

Hospitals can be very unsettling places. The sounds, smells, equipment, constant bustle, and all the sick people—including your mom—provide continual reminders that life is fragile.

You may find some members of your mom's medical team to be welcoming and understanding. Others may not be kid-friendly at all. They might lack the skills and compassion to communicate with young people, or they may be too rushed to take the time. If you encounter doctors or nurses who make you feel unwelcome or invisible, try not to take it personally. After all, you know what a great kid you are. Not getting to know you is their loss!

Make your mother's hospital room more pleasant by decorating it with photographs of family members and friends, artwork, and get-well cards. Give her a small tape player or CD player so you can listen to music together. You can make a tape recording of memories you share and give it to her.

These are activities you can do with your mom if she is feeling up to it:

- Tell her what's happening in your life
- Read books aloud
- Watch TV
- Play card or board games
- Record the family history
- Write a story together and then record it on video or audiotape
- Share a joke of the day
- Bring in a picnic meal so you can eat together
- Consult about homework
- Ask her for advice—moms usually love this!

What is an appropriate homecoming for my mother?

A clean house or apartment is probably the best gift you can give your mom. There are few things as demoralizing as returning to a messy home when you are feeling lousy. The most important rooms to put in order are her bedroom, the living room, bathroom, and kitchen. If you don't know where things belong just stack them in neat piles. Be sure to wash all the dirty dishes (including pots), wipe the counters clean, and take out the garbage. If you are pressed for time, vacuum only the dirtiest rugs. If your room is a disaster area, simply keep the door closed until you have time to straighten it.

Leaving the hospital may be upsetting for your mom. In the hospital her medical team took care of her and assumed responsibility for her health. Now her well-being is in her own hands, and that may seem overwhelming. She may not appear to be overjoyed at first to be home.

How can I help my mother when she is at home?

To help your mom return to normal keep her involved in your life. Let her know what is happening in school and with your friends. Say good-bye before you leave the house and greet her when you return. If you need adult permission to do something like visit friends, be sure to ask her.

New restrictions may be placed on you while your mother recovers. For example, she may ask you to keep the volume low when you play music or watch TV. Or she may ask you not to have friends over while she is resting. You may resent these restrictions—what teenager wouldn't?—but sometimes your mother must come first.

Try to anticipate your mom's needs so she doesn't have to constantly ask you to run errands. Bring her snacks, meals, cold or warm drinks, the newspaper, books to read, and so on. Help her write thank-you cards. If your family can afford a portable telephone, now is a great time to buy one if you don't own one already. You can bring the phone to your mom anywhere in the house.

If you feel comfortable cooking and cleaning up the mess afterward, either prepare your mom's favorite meals, or supplement packaged and takeout foods with a good, healthy salad. If someone else is looking after your mom and you aren't sure where you fit in, ask what you can do to help.

Once your mother starts her treatment program, try to establish a daily and weekly routine with your family. Make sure you understand your responsibilities. Try to be flexible! With so many unknowns in your life right now, your plans may fall through. Try to channel your disappointment constructively by making alternate arrangements.

How can I tell my mother I am being expected to do too much?

Helping out constantly can be wearing. It is normal to feel resentful of your mother for needing your help. But remember, she isn't deliberately acting helpless or lazy. Yelling at her will just make you both feel bad, so try to curb your temper. In case you don't, apologize as soon as you have cooled down.

If you feel overburdened, calmly talk to your mother or your father and negotiate a way to relieve the pressure on you. Now is the time to take up the offers of help that friends and neighbors have made. Make a list of your duties that can be handed over to others—at least for a little while. If your parents can afford one, suggest that they hire a temporary homemaker or home-health aide. You need to take breaks—visit friends, talk on the phone, veg out in front of the TV, or just get away for a short time.

Am I a selfish person if I forget about my mom for a while and have fun?

You are not a selfish person if you find the time and space for your own needs. Your mother knows it's important for you to have fun and be happy even though she may feel awful. You are entitled to moments of joy and laughter. These breaks will refresh you. Enjoying yourself does not mean you have stopped loving your mother. You need to find ways to have fun. Perhaps the whole family can brainstorm entertaining activities in which to participate together. Taking care of yourself is a necessity!

I get into trouble in school and rebel at home. What is wrong with me?

You are at that time in life—adolescence—when children break away from their parents. Sometimes your need to be independent clashes with your parents' desire to control. You may question and criticize your parents' values and behaviors. You may resent their attempts to tell you what to do. Add to this already turbulent situation the stress of breast cancer, and what happens?

You may fight more with your parents, siblings, and friends. You may get angry at your mom for being sick and then feel guilty about it. You may make a major production over a minor sniffle or a little pimple. Your classwork may suffer. You may be more tired, grouchy, and disorganized than usual. If your mother helped with your homework and no one fills the gap, you may slip behind.

Some of what's going on, however, may not be simple adolescent rebellion. Some kids in your situation break rules at home and in school in a subconscious attempt to attract attention. They may be feeling the loss of their parents' attention and may even feel rejected. An angry reaction from a parent or teacher may seem better than no attention at all. Misbehaving may be your way of saying, "Don't forget about me!"

It may also be a way of gaining control. You know if you act outrageously you will evoke an angry response. Some kids find it comforting to test limits and provoke a negative response. They feel more secure knowing that at least some things never change.

Other kids make scenes as a diversion. By stirring up trouble they distract the family from worrying about the cancer. This behavior is actually self-defeating because it only creates more stress.

Still others kids regress—they slip into behaviors typical of younger children. This is their way of saying, "I feel like a little kid. I want someone to take care of me."

Right now, life is hard for you. You feel different from your friends, and you don't see an end to it. How you choose to respond to this situation can make a difference. You need to learn how to handle stress and live with worry for a long time. Getting in touch with your feelings and expressing them can help you adjust better.

Is it okay to keep my feelings inside?

Some kids bottle up their emotions because they want to put up a strong front. They don't want to upset their mother by crying in front of her, especially if she has struggled to maintain a strong front herself. Others keep their feelings inside because they are afraid of them. Yet, to cope, you need to express your sad feelings. It's okay to cry. And it's okay for the family to cry together, too.

You need to share feelings with someone. You've heard this before—but are you listening? The best gift you can give yourself now is to find someone to listen to you and support you.

After cancer treatment ends will life return to normal?

Don't expect family life to return to normal the minute cancer treatment ends. Physically, your mom may still be weak and very tired. When she gets a burst of energy she may push herself too hard and become exhausted. For example, if the house became trashed while she was sick, she may want to tackle it immediately, and she'll probably expect you to help. In the middle of cleaning she may become so tired that she has to stop, but she'll expect you to finish the job! Do you see the potential for conflict here?

You may find your mother hard to live with as she learns her own limitations. She may be grouchier than usual and take out her impatience on the rest of the family. The most difficult adjustment may be adapting to new family roles. During your mother's illness you became more independent and made more decisions by yourself. Now your mother may want to return to the way it was, but you may be unwilling to give up your newly found freedom. Together you will need to work out new boundaries.

This need to become reacquainted with your mother may be quite upsetting, especially if you thought everything would be back to normal when she felt better. Adjusting to her recovery may be just as difficult as adjusting to her sickness! If the conflicts seem unresolvable, family therapy may provide solutions.

Believe it or not, as your mother's health improves you may discover that some good has come out of this whole experience.

- You may feel closer and more loving toward your parents and siblings.
- You may feel proud of your family's ability to cope under severe stress.
- You may have enhanced your appreciation for life and family.
- You may be more responsible and self-reliant.
- You may have become more understanding of the needs of others.
- You will be able to advise and comfort friends when bad times overwhelm their lives.
- You will have learned how to tackle difficult problems and find creative solutions for them.
- You will have gained the knowledge that you can face terrible situations and survive.

Will the cancer come back?

Breast cancer detected in the early stages can usually be cured, but more advanced cancers may reappear. The outcome can go either way, and this can make the years following treatment very difficult emotionally.

Worrying about whether the cancer has spread is only natural. Every time your mother reports for a checkup you may feel particularly anxious. You may feel frustrated when you ask about the possibility of a recurrence and the response is *we don't know.* Often that is the truth—no one may be able to tell you definitely whether your mother has been cured.

Doctors are armed with these statistics that may or may not apply to your mother:

- Sixty percent of the breast cancers that come back appear within the first three years.
- Another 20 percent of returning cancers occur within four to five years.
- Twenty percent recur in later years.
- Women who have had cancer in one breast have an increased risk of developing a new cancer in the other breast—about a 1 percent risk per year or an average risk of 15 percent over a lifetime. This is not a recurrence of the original cancer.

Living with uncertainty is one of the most horrible aspects of breast cancer. Some girls grow up with the sense that they could suddenly find themselves without a mother. For most, the worry decreases over time. But keep in mind that even if the cancer returns, more women are living with breast cancer than ever before and new treatments are continually being found.

Coping if the Battle Is Lost

This may be the most upsetting chapter of the book. It will not apply to you if your mother's cancer treatment has been successful. But sadly, some cancer treatments fail and cannot stop the spread of cancer.

If your mother is losing the battle to cancer, you may realize it deep inside even if no one has told you. You may have overheard a doctor's comment or something a friend or relative said. The information you gleaned from reading may have given you the clue. Or maybe you just plain know. If an adult hasn't confirmed your suspicions, ask. You have a right to know if your mother's illness is expected to result in death. Perhaps you are wrong and you are terrifying yourself needlessly.

But what if you are correct? To help you through this very difficult time, you may want to read and discuss this chapter with your father, a friend, or another adult you trust.

How long will my mother live?

If the cancer spreads, no one can tell you for sure how long your mother will live. Doctors can give you statistical averages that may or may not apply to your mother. These numbers tell you what happened to other women in the past. Like an old photograph they provide a good historical record but don't reflect the present. They fail to account for recent advances in cancer treatment and your mother's own unique situation.

The only certainty you have is that things will continue to change. You will continue to change and grow, just as you have grown and changed since your mother's cancer was first detected. If your mother has been sick for a while, you have already adjusted to living without her in many respects. You have become more independent.

Who will take care of me if my mother dies and I don't have a father?

This is a good question to discuss with your mother, if possible. She may already have asked someone to be your guardian. If so, her wishes should be protected by spelling them out in a will. A will helps to ensure that everybody will understand your mother's instructions. Find out if your mother has also made provisions for your financial support and education plans. If your mother has not chosen a guardian, ask her to consider it. Tell her whom you think could provide you with a secure and loving home.

If you can't talk about a guardian with your mother, make a list of all the people you and your mother love. These people know you are not old enough yet to live alone, and they would make sure you would be settled in a good home. It is scary but OK to think about life without your mother. All kids at some time or other imagine life without their parents.

Is it normal to withdraw from my mother and avoid her?

If your mother has been ill for a long time, her appearance may have changed so much that you find it hard to look at her, touch her, and give her hugs. Perhaps she moans or makes other unusual sounds. Maybe she has developed an unpleasant smell. All of these changes may repulse you and make you feel guilty for feeling that way.

Remember that inside that body is the same woman you have always known and who wants you to know that she loves you. When you were small, she took you by the hand when you needed help climbing stairs or crossing streets. Now she needs your help. Try to take her hand and look her in the eye when you speak with her. Let your mother know you love her. Try not to think about how she looks now.

Sometimes medication or illness can affect one's personality so much that you almost don't recognize her. If your mother is constantly cranky, sleepy, forgetful, or distant, it can be very frightening. Try to identify a time of day to approach her when she seems to be more of her old self. The changes in your mother's personality may be unpredictable. On good days she may be friendly and concerned—much like the old mom you remember. On bad days she may answer you with silence and turn away.

If your mother has withdrawn completely from you, it's time to talk to your father or someone you trust about what is going on. You need to know what is causing the changes and if the changes will go away. Remember, the old mom would never, never stop loving you. It is just the illness or the drugs that make her act the way she does.

What will happen if my mother is dying?

If your mother is dying, you may worry about how comfortable she is able to be. Taking care of her may be too great a burden for your family, even with the help of a nurse or health-care aide. She may require assistance just to eat, bathe, or relieve herself, and she may need to receive painkillers by injection or IV. If she cannot be cared for at home, a hospital, nursing home, or *hospice* may be the best possible place for her.

You may find yourself being incredibly angry with your mother for being so ill, and then you may feel very guilty about being angry at her for dying. This is a very common experience. Anger and guilt, as well as sadness, often spread themselves around when somebody is in the process of dying. Even your mother may feel angry and guilty about being so helpless and about leaving you before you are fully grown.

You may find it very frightening if your father and other adults cry or act totally out of character. Simply because they are adults doesn't mean they can be in control all the time. Despite their good intentions, they may not know what to do or say in this situation to help you. After a period of mourning when they have had a chance to reflect on your mother's life and death, they will find the strength to carry on. So will you. In the meantime, seek out other adults whom you trust.

What are the "stages of dying"?

During a terminal illness a patient may go through one or more of these five stages that were described by psychiatrist Dr. Elisabeth Kübler-Ross in her book *On Death and Dying*:

1. Shock and Denial—The patient is unable to believe that she is dying.

2. Anger—When the truth sinks in, she becomes angry. She realizes she's going to lose all the people she loves, as well as herself. Her rage may be vented on the people closest to her.

3. Bargaining—The patient tries to make a deal, usually with God or herself, to forestall death. She might make a promise like, "I'll never lose my temper again if you let me live until next spring."

4. Depression—The patient gives in to despair and grieves her own impending death.
5. Acceptance—Some dying people, but not all, make peace with themselves and with the world.

The dying person's family may also go through these stages. In addition, they may feel relieved when the patient dies because both her suffering and their own ordeal have ended.

What will happen to me if my mother dies?

Even if you know death is inevitable, it is still an awful shock when it happens. You may find it hard to accept. For a while you may feel numb, or you may hate your mother for dying and leaving you. Eventually you will feel the hurt of losing her. You will wonder if life will ever be normal again. The pain will gradually lessen, but your love for your mother will stay. Life goes on, and someday you will experience happy feelings again.

After losing a mother, you may worry that your father may also die too soon. The likelihood of both your parents dying while you are young is very, very slim. A good therapist can help you deal with your loss by giving you the chance to talk about your innermost feelings and concerns. Counseling may be especially helpful if you and your mother shared a stormy relationship or if your mother was mean to you at times. Your therapist or counselor can help you sort through both the good and the bad memories so you can eventually come to terms with whom your mother really was.

If you are adopted, you may have to deal with an extra issue. You may feel that you have been abandoned twice—first by your birth mother and then by your adopted mother. Counseling may help you come to terms with your losses and help you realize that you are not at fault.

Will my life ever be normal again?

Your life will become normal again, but it will be a different kind of normal, one without your mother. You will establish a new day-to-day routine.

Your mother will always be part of you. Throughout your life you will have reminders. When you are confused and in need of advice, you may think of her. When you have good news you want to share, you may remember her. As you grow older you may see your mother's features when you glance at a mirror or gaze into your children's eyes. Many of these reminders will spark wonderful memories that leave you smiling. Others will leave you sad and teary-eyed.

Some experiences may be especially difficult:

- Mother's Day with all its commercial messages.
- Watching your friends interact with their moms.
- Listening to friends complain about their mothers.
- Bumping into your mother's friends or coworkers.
- Seeing other mother-and-daughter pairs doing the things you long to do with your mother.
- TV shows, movies, and plays that feature the mother-daughter relationship.
- Adjusting to a stepmother if your father remarries.

Losing your mother is probably one of the most terrible things that can happen to you. But the important thing to know is that your life will go on. You will continue to grow and develop into a young woman with an exciting life of your own. You still can fulfill your dreams and be a good mom yourself someday. The knowledge that you can survive just about anything will be carried with you for the rest of your life.

What's in the Future?

Wouldn't it be great if cancer could be treated the way most medical problems are solved on *Star Trek?* The doctor could wave a medical tricorder over your body, and you would be cured instantly.

Researchers aren't promising an instant fix for breast cancer, but they are investigating better methods to detect, control, and prevent the disease. Someday, probably in your lifetime, breast cancer will no longer be a life-threatening condition. Recent advances raise the hope that a prevention or cure will be possible. Look for exciting developments in these areas of research:

- Genetics—identifying genes that can increase the risk of breast cancer
- Gene therapy—replacing defective genes with normal genes
- Chemoprevention—using drugs to lower the risk of breast cancer
- Drug development—improving existing treatments and developing new ones

- Tumor growth factors—controlling the molecules that permit and encourage cancer growth
- Immunology—making the body's natural defense against cancer more effective

Should I be tested for a mutated breast cancer gene?

Tests to identify carriers of the mutant BRCA1 and BRCA2 genes exist. Since most breast cancers are not caused by inherited mutations of the BRCA1 or BRCA2 genes, most women will not benefit from genetic testing.

However, women who have a significant family history of breast cancer, ovarian cancer, and prostate cancer may be carriers of a mutated form of the BRCA1 gene or BRCA2 gene. Carriers face as much as a 50 to 85 percent chance of developing breast cancer. They must also confront an increased chance of getting ovarian cancer.

Women over the age of eighteen in cancer-prone families need to consider the advantages and disadvantages of genetic testing. A blood sample is all that is needed. However, the lab test itself is extremely complex and may be quite expensive if your health insurance does not cover it. If you are thinking about genetic testing, discuss the ramifications of the test with a professional trained in genetics.

What are some of the pros and cons of genetic testing?

- *Genetic testing* can reveal whether or not you have a known mutation on the BRCA1 or BRCA2 gene linked to breast cancer. But the test cannot tell you if or when the cancer will appear. Some women with a mutated gene never develop breast cancer!
- A woman who tests positive carries a mutated gene. The results of her test may not remain private. Her

employer and insurance companies may gain access to the information. This may reduce her ability to obtain health, life, or disability insurance. She may also face job discrimination because some people may not want to employ or promote an individual who could develop cancer. It is hoped that, in the future, laws will protect individuals against discrimination for genetic disorders.

- Women who test negative do not carry a known mutated gene. However, the test cannot reveal if they have an unknown mutation, one that the test cannot detect but that may trigger cancer in the future.
- Women who test negative may gain a false sense of security because they believe they are safe from breast cancer. However, they still face the same risk as women in the general population.

What are my options if I carry the mutated gene?

Three major options exist at the time of the writing of this book. Women who know they have a mutated gene can choose to live with the risk and careful monitoring. They can opt for surgical removal of both breasts. Or they can try chemoprevention—taking medicines such as tamoxifen, *raloxifene*, or *fenretinide*—to lower the risk of breast cancer.

A double mastectomy greatly reduces the risk of breast cancer but does not eliminate it totally. Some breast tissue still remains behind after surgery, with a very slight chance that breast cancer could arise in it.

Women who choose to keep their breasts need to perform monthly breast self-exams and see their nurse or doctor at least once every six months for a clinical breast exam. Monitoring by mammography or possibly by MRI is also important. These measures cannot prevent breast cancer. But they usually catch cancer early enough so that it can be easily treated.

Tamoxifen has already been shown to be effective nearly half the time in preventing cancers from developing in the healthy breasts of women diagnosed with breast cancer. See pages 114–115 for more information on tamoxifen.

Researchers are studying the osteoporosis-prevention drug raloxifene for its effectiveness in preventing cancer in high-risk women. (Osteoporosis is a condition in which the bones become weak and brittle.) Raloxifene is similar to tamoxifen but produces fewer side effects. It is good for strengthening bones, too! Early test results show that it lowers breast-cancer risk by 75 percent. However, it can only be used by postmenopausal women—women who have stopped menstruating.

Fenretinide, a drug related to Vitamin A, is also being studied. It fights cancer by imposing order on cells that are growing out of control. In preliminary trials fenretinide sharply cut the risk of recurring cancers in young women, and it also reduced their risk of ovarian cancer. Fenretinide produces fewer side effects than tamoxifen, but so far it has been shown to be effective only in premenopausal women.

If you carry the mutated gene, seek out the most current advice available and go for counseling before you make a decision about treatments. By the time you read this, new preventive therapies and better choices may be available.

Will screening techniques improve in the future?

New technologies already in existence may make it easier to spot breast-cancer tumors in the future. *Digitized mammograms* can record X rays in computer code instead of making a picture on film. Special software can magnify tiny suspicious spots in the resulting computer image, making detection of very early cancer possible.

MRI scans can be customized to ignore cysts and fat, and to focus in on cancer. MRI technology may also revolutionize cancer surgery. A low-powered laser could be used to destroy cancer cells, while an MRI scan continually shows the surgeon where to aim the laser.

The *PET scanner* is a high-tech machine that provides images of the inside of the body. Like the CAT scanner and MRI, the PET scanner relies on computer technology. The acronym PET stands for *positron emission tomography*. A quick physics lesson may help you understand how it works:

Before undergoing a PET scan, a patient is injected with a solution of radioactive sugar. The sugar circulates throughout the body and is taken up by active cells. This special sugar gives off *positrons*—very tiny particles that are even smaller than atoms. When positrons meet electrons (the tiny particles surrounding the nucleus of an atom) they explode and give off radiation. The PET scanner detects and records the location of the radiation. Its computer translates this information into a picture. Since many tumor cells take up sugar faster than normal cells, the PET scan can disclose their location. It may be able to catch many of the breast cancers that mammograms miss.

What else is new in the area of screening?

Some scientists are exploring the use of light imaging to detect cancer. Tumors contain more blood vessels than the surrounding tissue, and so they reflect more red light. Also, because tumor cells are more active than healthy breast cells, they absorb and reflect light differently. The researchers hope to develop optical scanning devices to detect these differences. If it works, optical scanning will be safer than X rays and could be used with younger women whose breasts are too dense to be successfully evaluated by a mammogram.

Other researchers are striving to develop better tests to detect *tumor markers*. Tumor markers are substances that may appear in abnormal amounts in the blood, urine, or the fluid taken from the nipple of breast-cancer patients. Tests already exist for some tumor markers, but they are not reliable enough to be used routinely in breast-cancer screening.

In 1999, Australian scientists discovered a new way to test for breast cancer by analyzing hair. They found that if a woman has breast cancer, her hair growth is affected at the molecular level. By examining a single hair using a special X-ray technique, the scientists can diagnose breast cancer. They also found that the hair of healthy women carriers of the BRCA1 gene is also affected at the molecular level. This special X-ray technique can help poor women living in remote areas where mammography or genetic testing is unavailable. A sample of their hair could be sent to a distant lab where the testing could be performed.

In what other ways will research at the molecular level help?

Research at the molecular level holds great promise. Scientists are looking for a way to detect the first signs of abnormal change on the surface of breast cells. They hope to find cancer so early that the abnormal cells will have divided only a few times. A small biopsy could easily be performed to get rid of the cells and cure the cancer.

If scientists learn exactly how a normal cell turns into a cancer cell, they may be able to reverse the process. They may be able to find a treatment that turns cancer cells back to normal or a treatment that blocks precancerous cells and prevents them from becoming a fully developed cancer.

What new treatment options look promising?

A drug called *Arimidex* may be even more effective than tamoxifen in fighting advanced cancers in postmenopausal women. Arimidex works by suppressing estrogen production, so there is less estrogen available to fuel the growth of hormone-sensitive cancer cells. Arimidex is already used to treat advanced cancers that have not responded to tamoxifen. Studies are under way to see whether doctors should prescribe Arimidex to postmenopausal women as a first-line treatment instead of tamoxifen.

A class of drugs called *biphosphonates* may join the arsenal of weapons used to combat the spread of breast cancer. They have already been shown to reduce tumors that have spread to the bones. Researchers are conducting trials to determine if biphosphonates can also lessen the spread of cancer cells to the bones and to organs, such as the lungs and liver.

Noscapine, a cough suppressant sold in Sweden, Japan, and South Africa, may be not only an effective cough reducer but also a potent tumor killer. Researchers injected mice with human breast-cancer cells to produce large tumors. Then the mice were given noscapine. The noscapine stopped the tumor cells from dividing, and within three weeks the tumors had shrunk by 80 percent. For nearly thirty years noscapine has been used in the treatment of coughs. Additional research is essential to show whether or not it will make a powerful tool in the fight against cancer.

Researchers are testing the cancer-fighting potential of certain vitamins and some other naturally occurring chemicals in fruits and vegetables.

Can tumors be starved?

To grow larger than the size of a pea, a tumor must create its own blood supply. To do this, tumor cells release chemicals that cause new blood vessels to form. The new blood vessels bring oxygen and nutrients to the tumor, enabling it to expand and spread. Researchers are testing drugs to halt the growth of new blood vessels and starve the tumor.

Can resistance to cancer drugs be reduced?

Scientists may find a way to combat drug resistance in cancer cells. They know that a resistant cell manages to "pump" anticancer drugs out of itself. They also have discovered a gene that helps to make cancer cells resistant to anti-cancer drugs. Now the researchers are trying to find drugs that will block drug resistance. If they are successful, chemotherapy will become more effective.

What is immunotherapy?

Researchers hope that mobilizing the body's immune system will make a better weapon against breast cancer than chemotherapy and hormone treatments. You are probably familiar with how your immune system works. When harmful microbes sneak past the skin and enter body tissues, amoebalike white blood cells seek out the microbes and gobble them up. Other white blood cells—lymphocytes—aid in the fight. They recognize the distinct chemicals on the surface of each kind of microbe and produce a specific antibody to attack it. After the antibodies destroy the microbe, some antibodies stay in the bloodstream for years or even for life. These antibodies will rally in the defense of the body if the microbe invades again.

You probably wonder what this has to do with battling cancer. One kind of lymphocyte, called a *T cell*, identifies and attacks cancer cells before they have a chance to multiply. *NK cells*—short for natural killers—pitch in. T cells and NK cells destroy abnormal cells without harming healthy ones! They patrol the body like soldiers on the lookout for enemy invaders. Routinely, they detect and remove abnormal cells. Unfortunately, cancer cells sometimes grow undetected or reproduce so fast that the immune system cannot catch them all. Somehow the cells "cloak" their abnormality from T cells and NK cells and slip by them. Some kinds of white blood cells may turn traitor; they actually protect tumor cells from the onslaught of T cells and NK cells.

The challenge for scientists is to find a way to stimulate a patient's immune system to battle cancer. They are investigating three different vaccination strategies:

- a vaccine to prevent cancer
- a vaccine to immunize women against their own tumors to keep the cancer from spreading
- a vaccine to strengthen the immune system so it can better fight cancer cells

What are monoclonal antibodies?

Monoclonal antibodies are antibodies that have been produced in the laboratory. When injected into a patient, certain monoclonal antibodies can find and attach themselves to cancer cells. Scientists hope to fuse them with anti-cancer drugs that can be released when the antibody locates a cancer cell. These "smart bombs" would target and kill cancer cells while leaving healthy cells alone.

Monoclonal antibodies may also prove useful in:

- locating tumors so they can be treated with radiation
- alerting the immune system to attack by latching onto cancer cells
- thwarting the spread of cancer by binding to cancer cells and blocking growth signals

One of the most promising new treatments against breast cancer is the monoclonal antibody *Herceptin*. Herceptin binds with a molecule known as the HER-2/neu receptor, which is found on the surface of about 30 percent of breast-cancer cells. The receptor is involved in controlling cell growth. When it malfunctions, it gets stuck in the "on" position and fuels the growth of breast cancer. Herceptin turns off the receptor.

What does all of this mean for me?

Your generation will have a better chance of beating the odds against breast cancer than your mother's. Sometime in this century, detection will be possible at the very beginning stages of cancer development. Drug treatments will become less harsh and more effective. Mastectomies and lumpectomies will probably become obsolete.

In the meantime, you still need to protect yourself against breast cancer. If you have read Chapter Four you know what preventive measures to take against the disease. You also know what to do to detect it early. Now it's up to you to take charge of your health. As you grow older, keep yourself informed about new advances in the fight against breast cancer. The more you know, the greater your options will be. Try not to let the worry about breast cancer rule your life. Some research looks so promising that by the time you are thirty or forty years old, treating breast cancer may be as easy as treating an ear infection!

Antioxidants: Chemicals that protect against cancer.

Antiperspirant: A chemical applied to the armpits to reduce sweating.

Areola: A circle of darker skin that surrounds the nipple.

Arimidex: An anti-cancer drug used to treat advanced cancers.

Arteries: Blood vessels that carry oxygen-rich blood away from the heart to the tissues.

Atrazine: A commonly used pesticide that may pose a breast cancer risk.

Benign tumor: A tumor that is not cancer and does not spread to other parts of the body.

Beta-carotene: A yellow pigment found in the cells of brightly colored fruits and vegetables.

Biopsy: The surgical removal of tissue so it can be checked for abnormalities.

Biphosphonates: A class of drugs used to reduce tumors that have spread to the bones.

Bone marrow: The innermost part of bone where blood cells develop.

Bone marrow transplant: A controversial procedure in which the patient is treated with ultrahigh doses of chemotherapy so toxic that they destroy the bone marrow, and, it is hoped, the cancer. The patient is then given new bone marrow to rebuild the immune system.

Bone scan: A diagnostic test to determine whether any cancer has spread to the bones.

BRCA1 and BRCA2: Genes that appear to be responsible for many inherited breast cancers.

Breast reconstruction: An artificial breast constructed by a plastic surgeon to replace a breast removed by mastectomy.

Breast self-exam (BSE): An examination of the breasts performed by oneself.

Cancer: A disease of the cells resulting in uncontrolled cell reproduction. There are about one hundred different kinds of human cancers.

Capillaries: The smallest blood vessels.

Carcinomas: Cancers that arise in epithelial cells.

Carotenoids: Brightly colored particles found in the cells of vegetables.

Cell: The smallest living part of the body that can exist by itself.

Cell division: A process in which a full-grown cell divides into two new ones.

Cell membrane: The outer boundary of a cell.

Cesarean section: An operation for delivering a baby that involves cutting through the mother's abdomen and uterus.

Chemoprevention: The use of drugs to lower the risk of breast cancer.

Chemotherapy: A treatment that uses powerful drugs to fight cancer cells in the body.

Chromosomes: The threadlike structures within a cell's nucleus that contain genes and direct all the cell's activities.

Clinical breast exam: An examination of the breasts performed by a nurse or physician.

Colostrum: Liquid filled with antibodies to help a nursing baby fight infections. It is produced by the mother's breasts after a baby is born.

Computerized axial tomography (CAT scan): A device that combines X-ray and computer technology to make detailed pictures of the body's soft tissues and internal organs.

Cysts: Fluid-filled lumps that are almost never cancerous.

Cytoplasm: The fluid that surrounds the nucleus of a cell.

DDT: A pesticide that has been banned.

Deoxyribonucleic acid (DNA): Genetic material that is contained in chromosomes.

Diagnosis: The identification of a disease.

Dieldrin: A pesticide used widely on corn and cotton crops, and for termite control.

Digitized mammogram: A mammogram that is recorded in computer code instead of on X-ray film.

Discharge: A fluid that is secreted or released from the body.

Ducts: Tubes in the milk gland that lead from the lobules to the nipple.

Epithelial cells: Cells that line the milk ducts and milk glands, and cover the inside and outside surfaces of organs.

Estrogen: A female hormone produced mainly in the ovaries.

Fallopian tube: The tube leading from the ovary to the uterus.

Fatty acids: A fatty acid molecule is a chain of hydrogen, carbon, and oxygen atoms. Three fatty acid molecules make up part of every fat molecule.

Fenretinide: An anticancer drug that cuts the risk of recurring cancers in young women and reduces their risk for ovarian cancer.

Fiber: The undigestible carbohydrates found in plant foods.

Fibroadenoma: A smooth, round lump that is harmless.

Gene therapy: The replacement of defective genes with normal genes.

Genes: The structures on chromosomes that determine genetic traits.

Genetic testing: Tests to identify carriers of mutant BRCA1 and BRCA2 genes.

Glycerol: A compound that contains carbon, hydrogen, and oxygen. It forms the "backbone" of a fat molecule.

Herceptin: A monoclonal antibody that may block the spread of some types of breast cancer by binding to cancer cells and blocking growth signals.

Heredity: The passing of traits from parents to offspring.

Hormone: A chemical messenger made in one part of the body and transported to other parts through the blood. Hormones help regulate body activities such as growth, development, and reproduction.

Hormone therapy: A drug treatment that cuts off cell access to estrogen.

Hospice: A homelike treatment center that provides medical support and other care for terminally-ill patients.

Immunotherapy: Treatment to strengthen the immune system.

Infiltrating cancer: A cancer that has broken through the borders of surrounding tissue and invaded it; also called *invasive cancer*.

Inherited traits: Traits passed from parent to child through the genes.

In situ cancer: Very early cancer that has not spread to surrounding tissues.

Invasive cancer: A cancer that has broken through the borders of surrounding tissue and invaded it; also called *infiltrating cancer*.

Inverted nipples: Nipples that pucker inward.

IV: An abbreviation for *intravenous*. It refers to equipment that places medicine directly into the bloodstream. The IV consists of a tube attached to a plastic bag containing the medicine. The other end of the tube is placed directly in a vein and the medicine drips into the body.

Lobules: The milk-producing part of the milk gland in the breast.

Localization biopsy: The removal of a lump using a mammogram or ultrasound to guide the surgeon to the precise location of the abnormality.

Localized cancer: An invasive cancer that has spread to surrounding tissue but not to distant tissues.

Lump: A bump beneath the skin that can be felt.

Lumpectomy: The removal of a cancerous breast lump along with the rim of normal tissues surrounding it.

Lycopene: A red pigment found in the cells of ripe tomatoes.

Lymph: The clear, almost colorless part of blood that seeps into spaces between the body cells.

Lymph nodes: Glands in the lymph system that form part of the body's defense system against germs and other harmful substances.

Lymph vessels: Structures in the lymph system that carry lymph fluid. Lymph vessels have thin walls and valves, and are similar to veins.

Lymphocyte: A kind of white blood cell that fights infection by producing antibodies.

Magnetic resonance imaging (MRI): A technique that uses magnetism to produce an image of the interior of the body.

Malignancy: A cancerous tumor.

Malignant tumor: A cancerous tumor.

Mammary glands: Glandular organs that produce milk.

Mammogram: A low-dose X ray that gives a clear, detailed picture of breast tissue.

Mastectomy: The surgical removal of a breast.

Menarche: The first menstrual period.

Menopause: The time in a woman's life when her menstrual periods end.

Menstruation: The monthly discharge of the blood-filled lining of the uterus.

Metastasize: The movement of cancer cells from a tumor to a distant part of the body through the bloodstream or lymph system.

Microcalcifications: Deposits of calcium in the breast that show up as white specks on a mammogram and may be an early sign of breast cancer.

Milk glands: Glands in the breast that can produce milk.

Mitochondria: Cell parts in the cytoplasm that release energy from nutrients.

Modified radical mastectomy: The removal of the breast and all the underarm lymph nodes.

Monoclonal antibodies: Antibodies that have been altered in the laboratory.

Mutate: To change.

Mutation: A change in one or more genes that results in a new trait.

Negative nodes: Lymph nodes that are free of cancer.

Nipple: The small tip of the breast.

NK cells: Short for "natural killers"—white blood cells that attack cancer cells.

Noninherited traits: Traits acquired by an individual that were not passed on through the genes.

Noninvasive cancer: Cancer at an early stage that has not invaded surrounding tissues.

Noscapine: A cough suppressant that may make a potent cancer killer.

Nucleus: 1. The control center of the cell that directs all the cell's activities. 2. The dense, central part of an atom.

Omega-3 fatty acids: Fatty acids that may protect against the development of breast cancer.

Oncologist: A doctor who specializes in cancer treatment.

Organ: A group of different kinds of tissue that join together to perform a specific function.

Organelles: The tiny parts that are contained in a cell.

Ovary: The female reproductive organ that produces eggs.

Ovulation: The release of an egg every month.

Period: The time of menstruation.

Positive nodes: Lymph nodes with cancer.

Positron emission tomography (PET) scanner: A machine that relies on computer technology and emissions from positrons to provide images of the inside of the body.

Positrons: Very tiny particles that are even smaller than atoms. When positrons meet electrons they explode and give off radiation.

Precancerous growth: Abnormal cells that don't have all the characteristics of a cancer cell.

Predisposition: A tendency or susceptibility.

Premenstrual syndrome (PMS): Physical and emotional changes due to hormonal shifts that take place in the week preceding menstruation.

Preventive surgery: 1. The removal of the ovaries to eliminate the major source of female hormones in the body. 2. The removal of the breasts to significantly reduce the risk of breast cancer in women who carry a breast-cancer gene.

Primary tumor: The place where a cancer first develops.

Progesterone: A female hormone produced in the ovaries.

Prosthesis: An artificial breast that is worn externally.

Protocol: A plan of treatment.

Pubic hair: Hair that appears at puberty and surrounds the external genitals.

Radiation: The transfer of energy by electromagnetic waves; nuclear radiation results from radioactivity—the breakdown of atomic nuclei.

Radiation therapy: A treatment that uses high-powered, invisible rays to damage cancer cells and prevent them from reproducing.

Radical mastectomy: The removal of the entire breast, the chest muscles beneath the breast, and all the underarm lymph nodes.

Radioactive chemical: A chemical that gives off invisible radiation.

Raloxifene: A drug that strengthens bones weakened by osteoporosis that may also prove to be effective in fighting breast cancer.

Receptors: Structures on the surface of a cell that control the entry of estrogen.

Regional involvement: A cancer that has just begun to spread to other nearby tissues such as the skin or lymph nodes.

Remission: The apparent disappearance of cancer.

Resistant: Pertaining to cancer cells that are no longer harmed by anticancer drugs which worked before.

Risk: The chance of getting breast cancer.

Saturated fats: Fats that are solid at room temperature.

Screening: The examination of healthy people for early signs of cancer.

Secondary tumor: A tumor that develops at a site distant from the original tumor.

Second opinion: A consultation with an additional doctor.

Sexual intercourse: The act of putting the male penis inside the female vagina.

Simple mastectomy: The removal of the breast and the lining of the chest muscles.

Staging: A system used to describe how far a breast cancer has spread.

Statistics: Facts that are presented in a manner that provides numerical information about a subject.

Stereotactic localization biopsy: The removal of a lump using X rays and a computer to generate a three-dimensional image that guides the surgeon to the precise location of the abnormality.

Systemic treatment: A treatment that involves the whole body, such as chemotherapy or hormone therapy.

Tamoxifen: An anticancer drug that prevents breast-cancer cells from acquiring estrogen.

T-cells: White blood cells that identify and attack cancer cells.

Tissue: A group of cells that grow and work together.

Tumor: An abnormal growth of tissue. A tumor can be benign or malignant.

Tumor growth factors: Molecules that permit and encourage cancer growth.

Tumor markers: Substances that may appear in abnormal amounts in the blood, urine, or the fluid taken from the nipple of breast-cancer patients.

Ultrasound: The use of high-frequency sound waves to make outlines of structures in the body.

Unsaturated fats: Fats that are liquid at room temperature.

Uterus: The female reproductive organ that holds and nourishes a developing baby until birth.

Vaccine: A substance used to protect a person against a disease.

Veins: Blood vessels that return blood to the heart.

Visualization: A relaxation technique used to form a mental image.

Wartlike growths: Benign growths that can appear in the milk ducts near the nipple.

Weaning: The gradual reduction of a mother's milk supply.

Books

For information on handling sexual harassment, read *Safe, Strong, & Streetwise: Sexual Safety at Home, On the Street, On the Job, At Parties, & More* by Helen Benedict (Boston: Little, Brown, 1987).

For practically everything you need to know about sex, there is *Sex Ed: Growing Up, Relationships, and Sex* by Miriam Stoppard (New York: DK Publishers, 1997).

You may find these books helpful in changing your eating habits and getting fit:

- Abner, Allison, and Linda Villarosa. *Finding Our Way: The Teen Girls' Survival Guide*. New York: HarperCollins, 1995.
- Schwager, Tina, and Michele Schuerger. *The Right Moves: A Girl's Guide to Getting Fit and Feeling Good.* Minneapolis: Free Spirit Publishing, 1998.

Some good books that may help you deal with your mother's breast cancer are:

- Brack, Pat, with Ben Brack. *Moms Don't Get Sick.* Aberdeen, SD: Melius Publishing, 1990.
- Cohen, Barbara. *The Long Way Home.* New York: Lothrop, Lee & Shepard, 1990.
- Fine, Judylaine. *Afraid to Ask.* New York: Beech Tree Books, 1986.
- LeShan, Eda. *When a Parent Is Very Sick.* Boston: Little, Brown, 1986.
- Strauss, Linda. *Coping When a Parent Has Cancer.* New York: Rosen Publishing Group, 1988.

These books may help you understand the process of grieving. They may be available in your library:

- Bernstein, Joanne E. *Loss and How to Cope with It.* New York: Seabury Press, 1977.
- Grosshandler, Janet. *Coping When a Parent Dies.* New York: Rosen Publishing Group, 1995.
- Krementz, Jill. *How It Feels When a Parent Dies.* New York: Alfred A. Knopf, 1981.
- LeShan, Eda. *Learning to Say Good-by When a Parent Dies.* New York: Macmillan, 1976.

Internet

These organizations provide useful information on their Web sites. Most can also be contacted through their toll-free phone numbers.

Kids Konnected is an organization that offers support for kids ages three through seventeen who have a parent with cancer. It was started by eleven-year-old Jon Wagner-Holtz in 1993 after his mother was treated for breast cancer and he didn't have any peers to talk to. Kids Konnected maintains a hotline that is open twenty-four hours a day for kids who want to talk about what they are going through. The program is run by youth leaders under the direction of caring adult volunteers. Phone: 1-800-899-2866

www.kidskonnected.org

The Girl Scouts' breast-cancer awareness page lists suggestions for helping yourself and others. It also gives you the opportunity to tell about your experiences and read what other girls have said.

http://www.gsusa.org/girls/

Type "breast cancer" in the "Search-the-site" box.

Gillette Women's Cancer Connection provides information for cancer patients, as well as for families and friends of patients. Phone: 1-800-688-9777

www.gillettecancerconnect.org/

The Web sites of the American Cancer Society and the National Cancer Institute post up-to-date information on breast cancer. Intended for adults, they provide more technical data than Web sites designed for kids.

The National Cancer Institute's breast-cancer page:
cancernet.nci.nih.gov/cancer_types/breast_cancer.html
American Cancer Society's Breast Cancer Network :
www3.cancer.org/cancerinfo/load_cont.asp?ct=5

The Black Health Net is an excellent online source for health issues that affect the African-American community. After you access the main menu, click on "Women's Health" to obtain information on African-American women and breast cancer.

www.blackhealthnet.com

The Susan G. Komen Foundation sponsors the Race for the Cure, the largest series of 5K runs in the nation, to raise money for breast-cancer research and programs related to breast health education, screening, and treatment. Phone: 1-800-462-9273

www.breastcancerinfo.com/bhealth/

The Ontario Breast Cancer Information Exchange Partnership is a coalition of organizations in Ontario, Canada, that work together to share breast-cancer information. Phone: 1-416-480-5899

www.tsrcc.on.ca/obciep/bcinfo.htm

KidsHealth.org posts "A Teenage Girl's Guide to Breast and Pelvic Exams." It explains why you need them, what to expect from them, and why not to worry about them.

kidshealth.org/teen/bodymind/obgyn.html

Y-ME National Breast Cancer Organization provides information, support, educational programs, and telephone counseling. You can contact them through their hot lines. For English, call 1-800-221-2141; for Spanish, call 1-800-986-9505

www.y-me.org

Index

Page numbers in *italics* refer to illustrations.